WAVE OF SHOW
The Third World War and
the return of Christ

Odule Bitol

I dedicate this book to the world and every nation. I want to help you understand and update you on what's coming soon. Be ready and prepared and don't be caught off-guard. I did my part and I'm not responsible for you because I delivered the message I received from God through the dream He gave me. Peace and Love and may the Lord help you abundantly and save your soul in the name of Jesus. Author Odule Bitol.

Table of Contents

INTRODUCTION

This book, *Wave of Show*, reveals the plan and the future of how the spirit of death will accomplish his routine before his final destruction. The central theme of this book is the Third World War and the return of Christ, including Armageddon. The book projects and reveals how the angel of death soon will be in charge of sabotaging mankind's life. The waves of war, earthquakes, tsunami, and political conflict have started already. It is spreading little by little in front of our own eyes. The book contains predictions that have been revealed to the author, and now to you, about what is about to happen. The wave of currents always starts small, but then rises to a huge wave, until causing a big, final explosion. The end of time is closer than ever, and the Third World War is right before your doorstep. What will be future of humankind?

Let's travel together throughout this book to receive the divine provisions supplied from above. Pay close attention to what we have to say. I challenge you to increase your knowledge, more than what you already have, just like I challenged myself to bring you this knowledge from the reference of the Book of Books and scientific research. After reading this book, you will come to the decisive point: where you would like to spend your eternity, friend? What is coming isn't a joke and you need to think about it and be prepared for it.

Author Odule Bitol.

The beginning of everything

My friends, pay very close attention to what you are about to read in this book. After God created heaven and earth, the sea, and everything on it, everything was in perfect condition in the eyes of God. But throughout the progress and the devolvement process of the leadership of God Almighty in His Kingdom, the wave of sin was about to introduce itself in heaven. It will cross to planet Earth through time; and affect all of humanity. We would like to help you understand the portrait of Jesus, our Lord and Savior, and our Father God in Heaven, who holds the future in His Hands, from before the beginning of time to the end of the eternity.

God knew exactly what would take place in heaven and earth. Jesus, the eternal Son of God, saw Satan's fall, and Heaven. He brought the past from eternity to the present to give His disciples and us today a clue of what happened in heaven when God cast down the dragon with his rebel angels to earth. We don't know much about this war incident in heaven. One day, we will know all the details in the name of Jesus. Now, we just have a flash of what the Holy Spirit revealed to us, that we can understand…!

Luke 10:18: "And he said unto them, I beheld Satan as lightning fell from heaven."

Satan's falling from heaven is described in Isaiah.

Isaiah 14:12–14: "How art thou fallen from heaven, O Lucifer, son of the morning! *how* art thou cut down to the ground, which didst weaken the nations! 13 For thou hast said in thine heart, I will ascend into heaven, I will exalt my throne above the stars of God: I will sit also upon the mount of the congregation, in the sides of the north: 14 I will ascend above the heights of the clouds; I will be like the most High. 15 Yet thou shalt be brought down to hell, to the sides of the pit."

Ezekiel 28:12–18: "Son of man, take up a lamentation upon the king of Tyrus, and say unto him, Thus saith the Lord GOD; Thou sealest up the sum, full of wisdom, and perfect in beauty. 13 Thou hast been in Eden the garden of God; every precious stone *was* thy covering, the sardius, topaz, and the diamond, the beryl, the onyx, and the jasper, the sapphire, the emerald, and the car-buncle, and gold: the workmanship of thy tabrets and of thy pipes was prepared in thee in the day that thou wast created. 14 "Thou *art* the anointed cherub that cov-ereth; and I have set thee *so*: thou wast upon the holy mountain of God; thou hast walked up and down in the midst of the stones of fire. 15 "Thou *wast* perfect in thy ways from the day that thou wast created, till iniquity was found in thee. 16 By the multitude of thy merchan-dise they have filled the midst of thee with violence, and thou hast sinned: therefore I will cast thee as profane out of the mountain of God: and I will destroy thee, O covering cherub, from the midst of the stones of fire. 17 Thine heart was lifted up because of thy beauty, thou hast corrupted thy wisdom by reason of thy brightness: I will cast thee to the ground, I will lay thee before kings, that they may behold thee. 18 Thou hast defiled thy sanctuaries by the multitude of thine iniquities, by the iniquity of thy traffick; therefore will I bring forth a fire from the midst of thee, it shall devour thee, and I will bring thee to ashes upon the earth in the sight of all them that behold thee."

Isaiah 14 and Ezekiel 28 are two key passages in the Bible that refer specifically to the kings of Babylon and Tyree,. We believe they also reference the spiritual power behind those kings, namely Satan. We know that the angels were created before the earth (Job 38:4–7). Satan fell before he tempted Adam and Eve in the Garden (Genesis 3:1–14). Throughout, the angels were created as citizens of Heaven; and citizens of Earth citizens. Regardless of our nationality, we all have a homeland, and we all are citizens of a country and subject to the laws of that land. If you and I ever get in trouble for some reason, we will be judged according to the law and the constitution of the country we're from. It is quite unbelievable: heaven has its constitutional law; and earth has learned to project this from the first constitution of all.

Job 38:33: "Knowest thou the ordinances of heaven? canst thou set the dominion thereof in the earth?"

Do you agree, yes or no? Whether you agree or not, this is the fact. For sure brothers, I will not be a citizen of hell forever and ever. But I will be a heaven citizen forever and ever, in the name of Jesus. Join me in that declaration. Odule Bitol.

God keeps them out of heaven

The unexpected place where sin started his journey, was in heaven; and continued his mission down to planet Earth. God held Ex-Lucifer, Satan, the devil, the dragon, the old serpent, and his rebel friend angels who were involved with him accountable. He punished them for the crime they committed collectively. The father of lies gave birth to sin in the Kingdom of God and also on planet Earth.

Revelation 12:7–9: "And there was war in heaven: Michael and his angels fought against the dragon, and the dragon fought and his angels, 8 And prevailed not; neither was their place found any more in heaven. 9 And the great dragon was cast out, that old serpent, called the Devil, and Satan, which deceiveth the whole world: he was cast out into the earth, and his angels were cast out with him."

We have done some deep research in the Bible. It seems like Satan was cast out before humankind was created. Therefore, Satan's fall must have occurred somewhere after the time the angels were created and before he tempted Adam and Eve in the Garden of Eden. Whether Satan's fall occurred hours, days, or years before he tempted Adam and Eve in the Garden, Scripture does not say. Satan was waiting for the right perfect time to create trouble between our relationship with our Creator God. After God created the Universe, He warned Adam not to eat from the tree of the knowledge of evil and good. He warned Adam that if he did that, he would die in all integrity.

Let me give you a quick flash in the words of God; I hope you pick it up. Remember when the demon said to Jesus, "Have you come to torment us before?" The demon knew that they were in the presence of the son of the living God. The demon knew that Jesus was on a mission to planet Earth to restore humankind because we are His property, and we were created in His image...!

Matthew 8:28–32: "And when he came to the other side into the country of the Gergesenes, there met him two possessed with devils, coming out of the tombs, exceeding fierce, so that no man might pass by that way. 29 And, behold, they cried out, saying, What have we to do with thee, Jesus, thou Son of God? art thou come hither to torment us before the time? 30 And there was a good way off from them a herd of many swine feeding. 31 So the devils besought him, saying, If thou cast us out, suffer us to go away into the herd of swine. 32 And he said unto them, Go. And when they came out, they went into the herd of swine: and behold, the whole herd of swine ran violently down a steep place into the sea, and perished in the waters."

This is getting exciting. My dear reader, may the Lord provide me with sufficient knowledge and wisdom to help you understand the revelation of the words of God, and the provisions God made for us by revealing to us the truth about the Tree of Life and the Tree of the Knowledge of Good and Evil. Both are images of the outstanding characteristics of the eternity of God and death. And what will occur shortly has to come ahead. Each one of those identities reveals the truth of who they are and the mission that each one should accomplish. Light for life. Darkness for evil and death.

The Tree of Life is the eternal glory of God in heaven and earth. The Tree of Death is the eternal death in the world and hell. Remember my dear reader, positive and negative always occur side by side. But that doesn't mean they have the same mission. Each one has its function. Ex-Lucifer, in the Hebrew language, means angel of light. His accomplices, the rebel angels, received that message even before we made it to Earth! That same warning our ancestors receive in the garden from God; not to touch the tree of knowledge of evil and good. Because whoever touches it will be contaminated by sin and die in the eternal of hell. Let me back up what we're saying here with the scripture of the words of the living God.

Jude 1:6: "And the angels which kept not their first estate, but left their own habitation, he hath reserved in everlasting chains under darkness unto the judgment of the great day."

God doesn't have an exception of personality or preference when it comes to sin. Satan transmits to us the same, bad fruit of the knowledge of evil that he created with his own hand in eternity. He and his angels are tested by his own medicine, in eternity from the tree of death that they were not supposed to eat.

Let's clarify this confusion. When Satan approached Eve, it was not with a physical fruit. He convinced her to be like God, and she accepted the bad knowledge of that fruit.

Genesis 3:1–7: "Now the serpent was more subtil than any beast of the field which the LORD God had made. And he said unto the woman, Yea, hath God said, Ye shall not eat of every tree of the garden? 2 And the woman said unto the serpent, We may eat of the fruit of the trees of the garden: 3 But of the fruit of the tree which *is* in the midst of the garden, God hath said, Ye shall not eat of it, neither shall ye touch it, lest ye die. 4 And the serpent said unto the woman, Ye shall not surely die: 5 For God doth know that in the day ye eat thereof, then your eyes shall be opened, and ye shall be as gods, knowing good and evil. 6 And when the woman saw that the tree *was* good for food, and that it *was* pleasant to the eyes, and a tree to be desired to make *one* wise, she took of the fruit thereof, and did eat, and gave also unto her husband with her; and he did eat. 7 And the eyes of them both were opened, and they knew that they *were* naked; and they sewed fig leaves together, and made themselves aprons."

In heaven, the devil turned the angels against God. He did the same thing on earth. He turned humankind against the command of God in the garden. By eating from the tree of death, he transmitted the bad prescription of pride and jealousy. The wage of sin is death, as it says in Romans 3: 23; "For all have sinned, and come short of the glory of God."

Ezekiel 28:13–16: "Thou hast been in Eden the garden of God; every precious stone *was* thy covering, the sardius, topaz, and the diamond, the beryl, the onyx, and the jasper, the sapphire, the emerald, and the carbuncle, and gold: the workmanship of thy tabrets and of thy pipes was prepared in thee in the day that thou wast created. 14 Thou *art* the anointed cherub that covereth; and I have set thee *so*: thou wast upon the holy mountain of God; thou hast walked up and down in the midst of the stones of fire. 15 Thou *wast* perfect in thy ways from the day that thou wast created, till iniquity was found in thee. 16 By the multitude of thy merchandise they have filled the midst of thee with violence, and thou hast sinned: therefore I will cast thee as profane out of the mountain of God: and I will destroy thee, O covering cherub, from the midst of the stones of fire."

When Adam and Eve sinned in the Garden of Eden, God did the same thing with humankind: holding them accountable for their sin. He holds them accountable against His will and also punishes them for the action they did and keeps them out.

Genesis 3:23: "Therefore the LORD God sent him forth from the garden of Eden, to till the ground from whence he was taken." Odule Bitol.

Jesus, the Triumphant

But there is a great difference here between us and the devil and his angels who rebel against our Father God in heaven. Our triumphant Jesus is the father of the future and knows at all from end to end. He already has a restoration plan for us. No one in eternity has a clue of what will come to pass for the Universe and eternity. The provisions and the projection that God has made for us were above the understanding of the angels and mankind, but through the progress and process of time, everything started to reveal itself to us from the Book of Books. It opened itself up to us to understand God's purpose and revelation for us and the whole world from the beginning and before time.

Palms 8:1–8: " (To the chief Musician upon Gittith, A Psalm of David.) O LORD our Lord, how excellent *is* thy name in all the earth! who hast set thy glory above the heavens. ²Out of the mouth of babes and sucklings hast thou ordained strength because of thine enemies, that thou mightest still the enemy and the avenger. ³When I consider thy heavens, the work of thy fingers, the moon and the stars, which thou hast ordained; **⁴What is man, that thou art mindful of him? and the son of man, that thou visitest him?** ⁵For thou hast made him a little lower than the angels, and hast crowned him with glory and honour. ⁶Thou madest him to have dominion over the works of thy hands; thou hast put all *things* under his feet: [7]All sheep and oxen, yea, and the beasts of the field; [8]The fowl of the air, and the fish of the sea, *and whatsoever* passeth through the paths of the seas." Odule Bitol.

Ephesians 1:4–9: "According as he hath chosen us in him before the foundation of the world, that we should be holy and without blame before him in love: 5 Having predestined us unto the adoption of children by Jesus Christ to himself, according to the good pleasure of his will, 9 Having made known unto us the mystery of his will, according to his good pleasure which he hath purposed in himself:"

John 3:16: "For God so loved the world, that he gave his only begotten Son, that whosoever believeth in him should not perish, but have everlasting life."

Jeremiah 29:11: "For I know the thoughts that I think toward you, saith the LORD, thoughts of peace, and not of evil, to give you an expected end."

Jeremiah 1:5: "Before I formed thee in the belly I knew thee, and before thou camest forth out of the womb I sanctified thee, and I ordained thee a prophet unto the nations."

Isaiah 49:16: "Behold, I have graven thee upon the palms of *my* hands; thy walls *are* continually before me."

The Angels and Mankind

The spiritual realm was a complete discovery package. God knew exactly what was inside of those mystery packages that were sealed for eternity in His hands. God already knew how this great project of warfare in heaven would take place and come to pass, and change the history of eternity and the entire world forever. God was waiting for the right time to move forward with His agenda according to His precious will, to reveal the continuation of His heavenly mystery plan from the beginning, before anything took place in heaven and on Earth, through his son, Jesus Christ. God knew from the beginning what He was dealing with, concerning the near future of the eternity of time and also the planet Earth.

The kingdom of God must be cleaned up. The following grabbed my attention during doing research…! The Tree of Good and Evil is a symbolic portrayal, which stands for each one of those eternal authors' characteristics, of who they are in all, integrity, the projection, and their mission, from the beginning to the end. Jesus, the Son of the living God, in all of His glory and power and sublime love. The Tree of Evil is ex-Lucifer Satan, in all his malevolence. He was already projected to be the Tree of Evil without even knowing it. These heavenly provisions already existed in heaven, the Garden of the Kingdom of God. And each one of them also stands for the borderline of the life of God and the death of hell when Satan and his angels sinned against the holy of holy. One of the main reasons Satan and his complicity were kicked out was also to prevent them from eating from the Tree of Life. This ensured that their sin didn't live forever and ever in the realm of God. The Tree of Life was reserved and was not there for the sake of the angels but for the sake and purpose of humankind according to God's will.

Jude 1:6: And the angels which kept 1not their first estate, but left their own habitation, he hath reserved in everlasting chains under darkness unto the judgment of the great day."

Revelation 6:1–17: "And I saw when the Lamb opened one of the seals, and I heard, as it were the noise of thunder, one of the four beasts saying, Come and see. 2 And I saw, and behold a white horse: and he that sat on him had a bow; and a crown was given unto him: and he went forth conquering, and to conquer. 3 And when he had opened the second seal, I heard the second beast say, Come and see. 4 And there went out another horse *that was* red: and *power* was given to him that sat thereon to take peace from the earth, and that they should kill one another: and there was given unto him a great sword. 5 And when he had opened the third seal, I heard the third beast say, Come and see. And I beheld, and lo a black horse; and he that sat on him had a pair of balances in his hand. 6 And I heard a voice in the midst of the four beasts say, A measure of wheat for a penny, and three measures of barley for a penny; and *see* thou hurt not the oil and the wine. 7 And when he had opened the fourth seal, I heard the voice of the fourth beast say, Come and see. 8 And I looked, and behold a pale horse: and the name that sat on him was Death, and Hell followed with him. And power was given unto them over the fourth part of the earth, to kill with sword, and with hunger, and with death, and with the beasts of the earth. 9 And when he had opened the fifth seal, I saw under the altar the souls of them that were slain for the word of God, and for the testimony which they held: 10 And they cried with a loud voice, saying, How long, O Lord, holy and true, dost thou not judge and avenge our blood on them that dwell on the earth? 11 And white robes were given unto every one of them; and it was said unto them, that they should rest yet for a little season, until their fellow servants also and their brethren, that should be killed as they *were*, should be fulfilled. 12 And I beheld when he had opened the sixth seal, and, lo, there was a great earthquake; and the sun became black as sackcloth of hair, and the moon became as blood; 13 And the stars of heaven fell unto the earth, even as a fig tree casteth her untimely figs, when she is shaken of a mighty wind. 14 And the heaven departed as a scroll when it is rolled together; and every mountain and island were moved out of their places. 15 And the kings of the earth, and the great men, and the rich men, and the chief captains, and the mighty men, and every bondman, and every free man, hid themselves in the dens and in the rocks of the mountains; 16 And said to the mountains and rocks, Fall on us, and hide us from the face of him that sitteth on the throne, and from the wrath of the Lamb: 17 For the great day of his wrath is come; and who shall be able to stand?"

The Tree of Life is the fullness of the abundance and holiness of the eternity of God. Jesus wishes to gain humanity back again for the Father. The Tree of Life is one of the most beautiful powerful symbols in God's Word. Not everyone understands the revelation and the message God is transmitting to us. The tree of death is the fullness of the eternal of death and hell. When the Word of God talks about the tree of life and death, it does not talk of a physical tree. The Word of God talks about the presence of God and the presence of evil.

Genesis 2:9: "And out of the ground made the LORD God to grow every tree that is pleasant to the sight, and good for food; the tree of life also in the midst of the garden, and the tree of knowledge of good and evil."

Genesis 3:22: "And the LORD God said, Behold, the man is become as one of us, to know good and evil: and now, lest he put forth his hand, and take also of the tree of life, and eat, and live forever: 24 So he drove out the man; and he placed at the east of the garden of Eden Cherubims, and a flaming sword which turned every way, to keep the way of the tree of life."

Revelation 2:7: "He that hath an ear, let him hear what the Spirit saith unto the churches; To him that overcometh will I give to eat of the tree of life, which is in the midst of the paradise of God."

Genesis 2:17: "But of the tree of the knowledge of good and evil, thou shalt not eat of it: for in the day that thou eatest thereof thou shalt surely die."

This proves the demon already knew who Jesus was.

Luke 8:28: "When he saw Jesus, he cried out and fell before him, and with a loud voice said, What have I to do with thee, Jesus, *thou* Son of God most high? I beseech thee, torment me not."

Heaven was the perfect destination place for ex-Lucifer, Satan, and his angels, to exercise their free will with which they were created by God. The Earth also has been the perfect ground destination, a territory place for mankind to exercise the freedom and the free will they were given by God, to be tested and prove themselves.. Eternity's destiny was meant and designed to be that way: to reveal and let us understand who we are, and will be forever, to the end and for the future. Follow the Light and Holiness of Jesus, the Light of Light, and the Bread of Life! Odule Bitol.

Proverbs 16:4–6: "The LORD hath made all *things* for himself: yea, even the wicked for the day of evil. [5]**Every** one *that is* proud in heart *is* an abomination to the **LORD: *though* hand *join* in hand, he shall not be un-punished.** ⁶By mercy and truth iniquity is purged: and by the fear of the LORD *men* depart from evil."

When you throw a seed in the ground, time will reveal the true natural character of that seed, whether it is good or bad. We can reverse it; and say the same things for the angels and humankind. Heaven was the spiritual ground where the angels' true characters could grow and prosper according to the plan of God. The Earth has also been the ground test for us to prove our true nature, the character of who we are, and if we love our Father God in heaven in the name of JESUS. No matter who you are, you will have to prove your true identity of your destiny, whether you are Job, Father Abram, Jacob, Isaac, Moise, Daniel, Mordecai, Esther, King David, Nahomie, and Jesus. Just to mention those names only. Odule Bitol.

Matthew 7:19: "Every **tree** that bringeth not forth good **fruit** is hewn down, and cast into the fire."

Psalms 66:10: "For thou, O God, hast proved us: thou hast tried us, as silver is tried."

Psalms 17:3: "Thou hast proved mine heart; thou hast visited *me* in the night; thou hast tried me, *and* shalt find nothing; I am purposed *that* my mouth shall not transgress."

Proverbs 17:3: "The fining pot *is* for silver, and the furnace for gold: but the LORD trieth the hearts."

Whosoever you are, if you cross the line of the nature divine character of the order of the majesty of God, you will pay the price in the eternity of hell.

Nobody knows anything until He reveals it to us, and we are finally figuring it out, through the name of Jesus, and with the help of the Holy Spirit. What a lot of people don't understand is that nothing catches God by surprise. But the Mercy of God had a plan for us before the creation. God had everything planned, and under the control of generation and generation, which must come to pass and go other way to the eternity of eternity forever and ever. Odule Bitol.

Daniel 12:1–4: "And at that time shall Michael stand up, the great prince which standeth for the children of thy people: and there shall be a time of trouble, such as never was since there was a nation *even* to that same time: and at that time thy people shall be delivered, every one that shall be found written in the book. 2 And many of them that sleep in the dust of the earth shall awake, some to everlasting life, and some to shame *and* everlasting contempt. 3 And they that be wise shall shine as the brightness of the firmament; and they that turn many to righteousness as the stars for ever and ever. 4 But thou, O Daniel, shut up the words, and seal the book, *even* to the time of the end: many shall run to and fro, and knowledge shall be increased."

Ephesians 3:9–11: "And to make all *men* see what *is* the fellowship of the mystery, which from the beginning of the world hath been hid in God, who created all things by Jesus Christ: 10 To the intent that now unto the principalities and powers in heavenly *places* might be known by the church the manifold wisdom of God, 11 According to the eternal purpose which he purposed in Christ Jesus our Lord:"

Matthew 25:41: "Then shall he say also unto them on the left hand, Depart from me, ye cursed, into everlasting fire, prepared for the devil and his angels:"

The introduction of all from end to end

I don't know about you but I'm very proud to introduce you to my JESUS, my Lord and my Savior. The future of all the futures, the eternity of eternity, the peace of peace, who were already there from the beginning before time. The river of all the rivers. The stone of all the stones. Life of all the life and the bread of life. The salvation of all the salvations. The key to all the keys. The door of all the doors. Captain of all the captains, General of all the generals, The love of all the love. The lawyer of all the lawyers. The history of all the history forever. The nature of all the natures.

The chief of all the chiefs. The richest of all the richest from heaven and Earth. The Lord of all the Lords. The President of all the presidents, and the king of all the Kings. The savior of saviors. The key central of all the centrals. The priest of all the high priests, and the expert in all the experts. The knowledge of all the knowledge. The presence of all the presences; and the prince of all the princes. The mountain of all the mountains. The fire of all the fires. The lighting of all the lighting. The rain of all the rains. The Storm of all the storms. The wind of all the winds. The snow of all the snows. The meaning of all life and all the senses. The way of life. The answer of answers. The truth of truths, and the light of all the lights. The principal unity of all the unity forever and ever. The water of life and the sovereign of all the sovereigns. Name above all names, and all powers. The compassion of all the compassion. The pure blood of all the human blood. The wave of all the waves. The law above all the laws.

No one in heaven and Earth can ever be compared to His wisdom. God the FATHER GIVES TO JESUS HIS SON, AND THE HOLY SPIRIT; to match His intelligence forever and ever. When we study the Book of Life, very carefully, we can see clearly that the First War, the Second War, the Third War, and the ARMAGEDDON, which also will come to pass, are already included in that the provision package of those seven seals, that our master Jesus Christ reveals to us in the Book of Revelation through the Apostle John. So, you can have a better understanding of what we are saying to you! The program of God, our Father, was already made before the founding of the whole world. We are now just seeing the accomplishment and the result of the entire project of the planning of God. Odule Bitol.

Psalms 139:1–24: " **(To the chief Musician, A Psalm of David.) O LORD, thou hast searched me and known *me*.** [2]Thou knowest my downsitting and mine uprising, thou understandest my thought afar off. [3]Thou compassest my path and my lying down, and art acquainted *with* all my ways. [4]For *there is* not a word in my tongue, *but*, lo, O LORD, thou knowest it altogether. 5 Thou hast beset me behind and before, and laid thine hand upon me. 6 Such knowledge *is* too wonderful for me; it is high, I cannot *attain* unto it. [7]Whither shall I go from thy spirit? or whither shall I flee from thy presence? 8 If **I ascend up into heaven, thou *art* there: if I make my bed in hell, behold, thou *art there*.** 9 If I take the wings of the morning, *and* dwell in the uttermost parts of the sea; [10]Even there shall thy hand lead me, and thy right hand shall hold me. 11 If I say, Surely the darkness shall cover me; even the night shall be light about me. [12]Yea, the darkness hideth not from thee; but the night shineth as the day: the darkness and the light *are* both alike *to thee*. 13 For thou hast possessed my reins: thou hast covered me in my mother's womb. 14 I will praise thee; for I am fearfully *and* wonderfully made: marvellous *are* thy works; and *that* my soul knoweth right well. [15]**My substance was not hid from thee, when I was made in secret, *and* curiously wrought in the lowest parts of the earth.** 16 Thine eyes did see my substance, yet being unperfect; and in thy book all *my members* were written, *which* in continuance were fashioned, when *as yet there was* none of them. 17 How precious also are thy thoughts unto me, O God! how great is the sum of them! 18 If I should count them, they are more in number than the sand: when I awake, I am still with thee. [19]Surely thou wilt slay the wicked, O God: depart from me therefore, ye bloody men. 20 For they speak against thee wickedly, *and* thine enemies take *thy name* in vain. [21]Do not I hate them, O LORD, that hate thee? and am not I grieved with those that rise up against thee? [22]**I hate them with perfect hatred: I count them mine enemies.** [23]Search me, O God, and know my heart: try me, and know my thoughts: [24]And see if *there be any* wicked way in me, and lead me in the way everlasting."

The First War was the beginning, path, and announcement of the development of the Second War. The Second War was the announcement of the Third World War, which would lead to Armageddon and the end of the final destruction of humans in history. Odule Bitol.

Proverbs 8:1–36: "[1]**Doth not wisdom cry? and understanding put forth her voice?** [2]She standeth in the top of high places, by the way in the places of the paths. 3 She crieth at the gates, at the entry of the city, at the coming in at the doors. [4]Unto you, O men, I call; and my voice *is* to the sons of man. [4]**Unto you, O men, I call; and my voice *is* to the sons of man.** [5]O ye simple, understand wisdom: and, ye fools, be ye of an understanding heart. [6]Hear; for I will speak of excellent things; and the opening of my lips *shall be* right things. [7]For my mouth shall speak truth; and wickedness *is* an abomination to my lips. [8]All the words of my mouth *are* in righteousness; *there is* nothing froward or perverse in them. [9]They *are* all plain to him that understandeth, and right to them that find knowledge. [10]Receive my instruction, and not silver; and knowledge rather than choice gold ¹¹For wisdom *is* better than rubies; and all the things that may be desired are not to be compared to it. ¹²I wisdom dwell with prudence, and find out knowledge of witty inventions. ¹³The fear of the LORD *is* to hate evil: pride, and arrogancy, and the evil way, and the froward mouth, do I hate. **¹⁴Counsel *is* mine, and sound wisdom: I *am* understanding; I have strength.** ¹⁵By me kings reign, and princes decree justice. ¹⁶By me princes rule, and nobles, *even* all the judges of the earth. ¹⁷I love them that love me; and those that seek me early shall find me. ¹⁸Riches and honour *are* with me; *yea*, durable riches and righteousness. ¹⁹My fruit *is* better than gold, yea, than fine gold; and my revenue than choice silver. ²⁰I lead in the way of righteousness, in the midst of the paths of judgment: **²¹That I may cause those that love me to inherit substance; and I will fill their treasures.** ²²The LORD possessed me in the beginning of his way, before his works of old. ²³I was set up from everlasting, from the beginning, or ever the earth was. ²⁴When *there were* no depths, I was brought forth; when *there cwere* no fountains abounding with water. ²⁵Before the mountains were settled, before the hills was I brought forth: ²⁶While as yet he had not made the earth, nor the fields, nor the highest part of the dust of the world. ²⁷When he prepared the heavens, I *was* there: when he set a compass upon the face of the depth: **²⁸When he established the clouds above: when he strengthened the fountains of the deep:** ²⁹When he gave to the sea his decree, that the waters should not pass his commandment: when he appointed the foundations of the earth: [30]Then I was by him, *as* one brought up *with him*: and I was daily *his* delight, rejoicing always before him; [31]Rejoicing in the habitable part of his earth; and my delights *were* with the sons of men. [32]Now therefore hearken unto me, O ye children: for blessed *are they that* keep my ways. [33]Hear instruction, and be wise, and refuse it not. 34 Blessed *is* the man that heareth me, watching daily at my gates, waiting at the posts of my doors. [35]**For whoso findeth me findeth life, and shall obtain favour of the LORD.** 36 But he that sinneth against me wrongeth his own soul: all they that hate me love death."

The First World War lasted from 1914 to 1918. It was caused by the buildup of tension between countries. The three long-term causes were the formation of empires, the accumulation of armies and weapons, and alliances. The trigger cause was the assassination of Archduke Franz Ferdinand. One of the causes of World War I was that countries wanted to form empires. This is called *imperialism*. From the late 1800s, the power of an empire was judged by its size. Britain had the largest empire, with lots of territories overseas, such as India. People would say "The sun never sets on the British Empire" because there were British holdings all over the world, so it was always day in some part of the empire. The total number of military and civilian casualties in **World War I** was about 40 million: estimates range from around 15 to 22 million deaths.

What was the reason that led to the Second World War?

The **causes of World War II**, a global war from 1939 to 1945 that was the deadliest conflict in human history, have been given considerable attention by historians from many countries who studied and understood them. The immediate precipitating event was the invasion of Poland by Nazi Germany on September 1, 1939, and the subsequent declarations of war on Germany made by Britain and France, but many other prior events have been suggested as ultimate causes. Primary themes in historical analysis of the war's origins include the political takeover of Germany in 1933 by Adolf Hitler and the Nazi Party; Japanese militarism against China, which led to the Second Sino-Japanese War; Italian aggression against Ethiopia, which led to the Second Italo-Ethiopian War and Germany's initial success in negotiating the Molotov–Ribbentrop Pact with the Soviet Union to divide the territorial control of Eastern Europe between them. Wikipedia. An estimated total of 70–85 million people perished, or about 3% of the 2.3 billion (est.) people on Earth in 1940. Deaths directly caused by the war (including military and civilian fatalities) are estimated at 50–56 million, with an additional estimated 19–28 million deaths from war-related disease and famine.

It will be no different for the Third World War.

The point and the message that I would like to relay here is that humankind never learns from the mistakes they made before. We always fall into the same trap as the devil set for us in the same matter. The same cause that caused the First World War and the Second World War is the same thing we are seeing now right before our own eyes. It will be the same cause that start the Third World War and lead to Armageddon, believe it or not. Odule Bitol.

The beginning of a war and the end never brought a good result, but always pestilence combined with disease. Thank God, I'm alive today. I can tell you what happened, after the earthquake in 2010 in Haiti. Pestilence was everywhere and it was not pretty. What happened in the First and the Second World Wars was more horrible than anything else on planet Earth. I can tell you for sure that the Third World War and AMAGEDDON will be more than the first one and the second one. And nothing will be compared to them forever and ever. In those wars from the past, the men who caused them were not equipped like we are today. Today, we have more chemicals of destruction material than material to protect humanity. No one can project the outcome of what will happen when that ugly day happens – nothing but destruction and sorrow.

Let's read what happened during the Spanish flu after the First World War. The Spanish flu pandemic of 1918–1919 was the deadliest in world history, infecting some 500 million people across the globe—roughly one-third of the population—and causing up to 50 million deaths, including some 675,000 deaths in the United States alone. The disease, caused by a new variant of the influenza virus, was spread in part by troop movements during World War I. Though the flu pandemic hit much of Europe during the war, news reports from Spain weren't subject to wartime censorship, so the misnomer "Spanish flu" entered common usage. With no vaccines or effective treatments, the pandemic caused massive social disruption: Schools, theaters, churches, and businesses were forced to close, citizens were ordered to wear masks and bodies piled up in makeshift morgues before the virus ended its deadly worldwide march in early 1920. bodies piled up in makeshift morgues. history.com/news/Spanish-flu-pandemic-death

The outbreak of the infectious respiratory disease known as COVID-19 triggered one of the deadliest pandemics in modern history. COVID-19 claimed nearly 7 million lives worldwide. In the United States, deaths from COVID-19 exceeded 1.1 million, nearly twice the American death toll from the 1918 flu pandemic. The COVID-19 pandemic also took a heavy toll economically, politically, and psychologically, revealing deep divisions in the way that Americans viewed the role of government in a public health crisis, particularly vaccine mandates. While the United States downgraded its "national emergency" status over the pandemic on May 11, 2023, the full effects of the COVID-19 pandemic will reverberate for decades.

history.com/news/covid/pandemic-death

More than two thousand years ago, the truth of truth and the three in one and the first of all forever and ever was sent to restore humankind from sin and reconcile us with our Father God in heaven. He said those powerful words when He was here on earth with us in the center of JE-RUSALEM, that today will be the capital of the Jewish nation. He told His disciples that I'm closer than ever. Odule Bitol.

The Destruction of Jerusalem

Israel is surrounded by its enemy from the north, south, east, and west. We can see it is happening right before our own eyes already. Please remember Israel in your prayers, because they need it more than ever. The nation of Israel is the chosen people of God Almighty. At this moment, the world r is turning against Israel. There is no doubt that the United Nations already has its agenda for the universe. They are always looking forward to the future for the opportunity to accomplish its mission. It will not be pretty. What do you think that mission would be: one world order?

The final hours have come, when everything will get ugly faster than we could imagine. Friend, wake up from your spiritual sleep. It hurts a lot when you see everyone else turning against you; 143 nations around the world have voted against the chosen people of God because they were only defending their rights. Haiti, a member and founder of the United Nations, have been pleading with them for help and never has done anything about it. Because they are selfish and work for themselves, and not for the people, but instead against the country and the people, and profit from the sorrow of the people whom they are supposed to be helping. I will not be quiet until God allows me to talk about especially, what is happening in the world the Bible says, that if you know the truth the truth will, set you free. No doubt out in the UN, there are good people there, but it doesn't make much difference if you are hanging out with the bad Apple.

On May 10, 2024, the United Nations General Assembly passed a resolution that recognizes Palestine as a member state and grants it added rights. The resolution includes the right to be seated with member states, introduce proposals and agenda items, and take part in committees, but does not grant Palestine the right to vote. The resolution passes with 143 countries in favor, nine against, and 25 abstaining. The upgrades will go into effect at the next session of the UN General Assembly on September 10, 2024. Wikipedia...

Blessings, to all of those nations who bless Israel. Genesis 12:3: "And I will bless them that bless thee, and curse him that curseth thee: and in thee shall all families of the earth be blessed."

We thank God for allowing my country, Haiti, to play a key role in the participation of the establishment of Israel as a nation within the international community. On May 14, 1948, in Tel Aviv, Jewish Agency Chairperson David Ben-Gurion proclaimed the State of Israel, setting up the first Jewish state in 2,000 years. Ben-Gurion became Israel's first premier.

Luke 21:10–24: "Then He said to them, Nation will rise against nation, and kingdom against kingdom. 11

And there will be great earthquakes in various places, and famines and pestilences, and there will be fearful sights and great signs from heaven. 12 But before all these things, they will lay their hands on you and persecute you, delivering you up to the synagogues and prisons. You will be brought before kings and rulers for My name's sake. 13 But it will turn out for you as an occasion for testimony. 14 Therefore settle it in your hearts not to meditate beforehand on what you will [f] answer; 15 for I will give you a mouth and wisdom which all your adversaries will not be able to contradict or resist. 16 You will be betrayed even by parents and brothers, relatives and friends; and they will put some of you to death. 17 And you will be hated by all for My name's sake. 18 But not a hair of your head shall be lost. 19 By your patience possess your souls. 20 But when you see Jerusalem surrounded by armies, then know that its desolation is near. 21 Then let those who are in Judea flee to the mountains, let those who are in the midst of her depart, and let not those who are in the country enter her. 22 For these are the days of vengeance, that all things which are written may be fulfilled. 23 But woe to those who are pregnant and to those who are nursing babies in those days! For there will be great distress in the land and wrath upon this people. 24 And they will fall by the edge of the sword, and be led away captive into all nations. And Jerusalem will be trampled by Gentiles until the times of the Gentiles are fulfilled."

The Third World War is right at your doorstep

We can see the war between Israel, Palestine, Iran, Iraq, and Syria and all the Arab country nations that surround the Israelite country. It is not a joke, and we're closer than ever. More than ever, we need to be ready at all costs and be close to our Savior. The Third World War is right at your doorstep. Jesus our Lord declared with his mouth when you saw Israel so rounded to be attacked by his enemy who is God's hatred, and the Jewish people. The return of Jesus Christ is closer than ever, so get ready. This is not like Hollywood. It's not an apocalypse movie we see in the theater or and TV. We can't compare what is coming with anything that we can imagine. It will be behind our understanding and nothing we have ever seen before.

Matthew 24:1–14: "And Jesus went out, and departed from the temple: and his disciples came to *him* for to show him the buildings of the temple. 2 And Jesus said unto them, See ye not all these things? verily I say unto you, There shall not be left here one stone upon another, that shall not be thrown down. 3 And as he sat upon the mount of Olives, the disciples came unto him privately, saying, "Tell us, when shall these things be? and what *shall be* the sign of thy coming, and of the end of the world? 4 And **Jesus answered and said unto them,**

Take heed that no man deceive you. 5 For many shall come in my name, saying, I am Christ; and shall deceive many. 6 And ye shall hear of wars and rumors of wars: see that ye be not troubled: for all *these things* must come to pass, but the end is not yet. 7 For nation shall rise against nation, and kingdom against kingdom: and there shall be famines, and pestilences, and earthquakes, in diverse places. 8 All these *are* the beginning of sorrows. 9 Then shall they deliver you up to be afflicted, and shall kill you: and ye shall be hated of all nations for my name's sake. 10 And then shall many be offended, and shall betray one another, and shall hate one another. 11 And **many false prophets shall rise, and shall deceive many.** 12 And because iniquity shall abound, the love of many shall wax cold. 13 But he that shall endure unto the end, the same shall be saved. 14 And this gospel of the kingdom shall be preached in all the world for a witness unto all nations; and then shall the end come.

Please prepare our souls to be ready when that trumpet sounds to make it with our LORD on the first trip.

Jeremiah 1:5: "Before I formed thee in the belly I knew thee; and before thou camest forth out of the womb I sanctified thee, and I ordained thee a prophet unto the nations."

I challenge you and then ask you this question: did God know you before anything did take place in the whole world; yes or no?? I will leave it to you friend! Always remember that when God Almighty was building the program and the project of the whole world, He already knew you and who you would be before Him.

Ecclesiastes 1:9: "The thing that hath been, it is that which shall be; and that which is done is that which shall be done: and there is no new thing under the sun."

Ecclesiastes 1:10: "Is there anything whereof it may be said, See, this is new? it hath been already of old time, which was before us."

Proverbs 8:17: "**I love them that love me, and those that seek me early shall** find me."

Jeremiah 33:3 "Call unto me, and I will answer thee, and show thee great and mighty things, which thou knowest not."

What a lot of people don't understand is that nothing caught God by surprise. The Mercy of God had everything already figured out before even the creation took place. He had everything already planned and under control before anything did take place in eternity. God had everything planned from the beginning for generations and generations that must happen.

Ecclesiastes 1:4: "*One* generation passeth away, and *another* generation cometh: but the earth abideth forever."

Isaiah 45:12: "I have made the earth, and created man upon it: I, *even* my hands, have stretched out the heavens, and all their host have I commanded."

Jeremiah 29:11: "For I know the plans I have for you," declares the LORD, "plans to prosper you and not to harm you, plans to give you hope and a future."

The world is out of control

The world will not improve from the state it finds itself in now. Instead, we will only get worse until we reach the destination of destruction as the Bible predicted it. That would lead the world to the worst of the worst in human history. If any country is better or more stable now, or if its people are doing better, than another country, it is not because you are the best on planet Earth, and have everything figured out or under control. No, no one does.

Isaiah 45:12: "I have made the earth, and created man upon it: I, *even* my hands, have stretched out the heavens, and all their host have I commanded."

But God does. Nobody has anything under control. If you have something under control for the moment, it is because God Almighty has allowed it. It will not last longer because the final day, the prophecy of the end of time in the Bible, will soon arrive. Those evil agents, of Satan, men and women, their game will be over. They have surrendered their hearts to the adversary of God, to Satan. They have turned against the will of the Lord of the Lords, the owner of eternity and the planet Earth. Note my words, friend, specially to you who are reading this precious book.

Those types of people we just mentioned love pleasure and love to serve the dark side. Not even thinking for a minute and measuring the consequences that they will be facing if they don't repent from the wicked evil. They will end in hell for their action.

We can see now how some of them reveal themselves when you were not expecting it. They go wild every time they find the occasion they were looking for. But sooner or later, it will come to pass and everything will fall apart. And that day is not so far away. We can already see the war between Ukraine, Russia, Israel, Palestine, Iran, and the Arab neighboring nations against Israel. There is war everywhere on earth. This has touched the trigger alert of the fire spark of the Third World War.

Think about NATO and the United States getting involved in the Ukraine war conflict, and China, waiting for the right opportunity to invade Taiwan... Israel and Palestine, Iran... and North Korea against the south of Korea. Do you think this is an accident? NO. This is not an accident. This is the preparation for the accomplishment path of the words of the living God. You may not be paying attention because you might be so busy and worrying about the material world to provide for your family and your needs. Nothing is wrong with that, but please don't ignore the warning you are receiving throughout this book. This is not the right period to waste time. From now on remember, my dear reader, time is very valuable. You can use it to provide for your needs, but also use it to provide for your soul. The ugly, dark moments that are approaching are not pretty or a joke. Soon we will face a very serious hour.

We are living in a time where people who were enemies will pretend to be partners or friends with one another. The reality here is not true at all. The true nature of this goal is political gain to try to achieve their agenda. But it will not last! At the end of the process, they will turn against one another. Read it for yourself in Revelation.

Revelation 17:17: "For God hath put in their hearts to fulfill his will, and to agree, and give their kingdom unto the beast until the word of God shall be fulfilled."

This project is the result of a deep, fundamental research into the Bible and history. This a quick reminder of what God has been saying over and over through his Living Word. He continues to say the same thing. We should learn lessons from history, but unfortunately, humankind never learns from the past because they are so hardheaded.

The strength of this powerful material is built on the provisions of a dream I received from God Almighty in the name of Jesus through the Holy Spirit. This roadmap book is the most important ingredient to help you and your family establish a solid foundation for your soul and your relationship with God. That's designed to teach you what's about to occur in these coming seasons.

Unbelievably, we will continue to see a lot of things in our generation. Let me give you a quick overview of what has already happened previously and present.

- The invasion of Panama and the capture of General Manuel Antonio Noriega, on 3 January 1990.
- President Jean-Bertrand Aristide, the coup d'état on 30 September 1991, and his return in 1994
- Pablo Escobar, executed on 2 December 1993, the head of the cartel of Colombia.
- The military operation by Chavín de Huantar on 22 April 1997, where hostages were rescued from the Japanese embassy.
- The terrorist attack on the World Trade Center in New York City on 11 September 2001.
- We saw the third millennium spanning the years 2001 to 3000 (21st to 30 centuries).
- President Saddam Hussein was executed on 30 December 2006.
- Osama bin Laden, executed on 2 May 2011, was the head of the terrorists in the Middle East region and around the world.
- Execution of President Muammar Gaddafi on 20 October 2011.
- The wave following the magnitude 7.0 earthquake in Haiti killed more than 300,000 people. I was there when it happened…
- The assassination of the president of Haiti (Jovenel Moïse) in his residence on 7 July 2021 shook the world.

- Japan earthquake and tsunami, leading to the death of 15.899 people and a material loss of over USD 360 billion.
- Ebola virus, Coronavirus 19, Etc.
- The celebrations of the independence of Haiti, the United States of America, Spain, France, Canada, Russia, England, China, etc.

This is just a quick overview of what has already happened in the world and has captured our attention in our generation. I hope you got it; we have seen more things than any other generation.

None of the things we mentioned in this list will be comparable to what is about to be unleashed on Earth. We're writing this book with a lot of sacrifice and putting it in your hands for you to have and keep it as a treasure, especially for those who love to be reading books. One day you will need something you can put your hand on as a guide.

After all our research we concluded with the help of the SPIRIT OF THE LIVING GOD, we know that the title "Wave of show" was given to me through A DREAM from God Almighty...! It reveals the wave of current, trouble, and calamity that will occur in those last outcoming days that is soon to come, like when you look at yourself in a mirror. The current political climate around the world gives the greatest Wave of Show. We haven't experienced this before, and neither have the generations before us.

The gloomy leaders who form part of this catastrophic satanic program we are talking about here, are some of those evil politicians and organizations who are supposed to stand for us all over the world...! Who is supposed to oversee the program of leadership of the world, for man's safety? Instead, they are the experts and authors of all the confusion that is going on right now on planet Earth. The reality is they don't care for nobody, but they are self and also don't understand the real plan of God for humanity. What is about to come our way, even our great grandfathers haven't ever seen something like this before a generation.

Like it or not it's our turn now to face parts of some of those sorrows that will come our way shortly in our generation's time, one way or another. We must pray to God to help us... for whatever situation we must face as a challenge when that time comes our way. Let's start praying to GOD ahead of time for our children, sons, daughters, and grandchildren, for God to protect them from whatever will come through our way in Jesus' name. From this horrible miserable wave of darkness that is already moving forward to reach its destination to ruin the world.

Wave of Show

Before Creation, the Earth didn't have any form. The Spirit of God, the living water, the way of life, the water above all the water of waters, was floating in the face of the water. On many occasions, we would like to have an idea about how everything took place, and what the place looked like in the beginning. Bringing the past of the creation to the present, after the deluge, we can have the perfect picture of when the Ark of Noah was floating in the water. There was nothing but only water in that moment, that was in existence. Putting it all together with the help of "ALL IN ONE," we concluded also this is how the universe looked like before the creation! In the time of the deluge, God decided to reset the Earth, put everything back to where it was from the beginning, and update it one more time with Noah's family and the animals that were with them.

Why is there more water than land in the world? In the beginning, the Spirit of God was floating in the water which means they were no land yet that existed, God decided to create the Earth. Logically, the Earth is surrounded by water from end to end.... Seeing God floating on the water and walking on it represents God predicting the future of each nation and country that will form in the world all in one.

Where did all those people come from, floating on the top of the water in the sea? Revelation 17:15 says all those people come from the same water that we saw the Spirit of God was floating in before the creation. Before anything took place from heaven and Earth, God knew who we were. We were all born from that water, and were transported into the physical land that God created for mankind to live peacefully and move forward, and to enjoy life where God planned it for us.

Jeremiah 1:5: "Before I formed thee in the belly I knew thee, and before thou camest forth out of the womb I sanctified thee, and I ordained thee a prophet unto the nations."

Everything was already running before we even came into existence. God, the Lord of the Lords, doesn't follow man's protocol but man follows his...! Water is the symbol and logo of life. The water gave birth to the earth and each one of us! When we look deep and very closely at it, we can see what the book of Revelation is describing here to us, through Apostle John. The multitudes of people he saw in the water prove one thing. When God Almighty was floating and navigating in the water it means He already was going through those people to form them as a nation.

The Bible said that the multitudes of people that John saw in the water were of different nations and spoke different languages.

Revelation 17:15: "And he saith unto me, the waters which thou sawest, where the whore sitteth, are peoples, and multitudes, and nations, and tongues."

Psalms 93:4: "The LORD on high *is* mightier than the noise of many waters, *yea, than* the mighty waves of the sea."

The entire ocean, containing 97% of Earth's water, spans 70.8% of Earth's surface,[8] making it Earth›s global ocean or *world ocean*.[23][25] This makes Earth, along with its vibrant hydrosphere a "water world"[43][44] or "ocean world",[45][46] particularly in Earth's early history when the ocean is thought to have possibly covered Earth completely.[41] The ocean's shape is irregular, unevenly dominating the Earth's surface. This leads to the distinction of the Earth's surface into a water and land hemisphere, as well as the division of the ocean into different oceans.

Seawater covers about 361,000,000 km^2 (139,000,000 sq mi) and the ocean's furthest pole of inaccessibility, known as "Point Nemo", in a region known as the spacecraft cemetery of the South Pacific Ocean, at 48°52.6′S 123°23.6′W. This point is roughly 2,688 km (1,670 mi) from the nearest land.[47] Wikipedia

Genesis 1:2: "And the earth was without form, and void; and darkness *was* upon the face of the deep. And the Spirit of God moved upon the face of the waters."

Genesis 1:9–10: "And God said, Let the waters under the heaven be gathered together unto one place, and let the dry *land* appear: and it was so.10 And God called the dry *land* Earth; and the gathering together of the waters called he Seas: and God saw that *it was* good."

On Sunday morning, 15 April 2018, at about 5:00 am, I was in my pastor's *territory,* in the missionary camp in the State of Mississippi, Lucedale. It is a place where this man of God has built and prepared to help and teach the word of God to local and international missionaries. A beautiful peaceful and safe place where you can pray, meditate, and talk to our Godfather in heaven, and learn a lot in Jesus' name.

I had a great dream there that I will never forget as long as I'm in our life. I saw a great tall mountain of a wave in the sea. The wave was making noise as usual when it's on its natural action, and you hear that noise going back and forth, and the wave was spreading and sprinkling everywhere like when it is hitting in the stone. I have never experienced something like this before in my life. There were a multitude of people at the top of it, and the wave rolled over with all of them; and taking them away. I didn't see them again. And I heard a powerful, audible very LOUD voice, that came from heaven; that SAID: WAVE OF SHOW…!

This is a tough title and subject; but at the same time this is what makes the value and the strength of this book, and the movie...! Please be patient; pay attention and read slowly because we are about to take you to another dimension from Earth to Heaven and from Heaven to Earth. What I mean is that we will be using the divine geographic map of heaven and the one from earth, so you can have a better understanding of the projection of this book.

Job 38:33: **"Knowest thou the ordinances of heaven? canst thou set the dominion thereof in the earth?"**

John 3:31: "He that cometh from above is above all: he that is of the earth is earthly, and speaketh of the earth: he that cometh from heaven is above ..."

Let us pray to our Father God in Heaven, the Creator of all, Heaven and Earth. We bow before your presence and your majesty. We beg you please and ask you to unlock our minds and help us to understand and receive the provisions you have sent to us in this book. We pray to you in Jesus' name. Amen!

Jeremiah 47:2: "Thus, saith the Lord; Behold, waters rise out of the north, and shall be an overflowing flood, and shall overflow the land, and all that is therein; the city, and them that dwell therein: then the men shall cry, and all the inhabitants of the land shall howl."

Real Dream

Regardless of what you are doing in life, the is always a positive position and a negative choice, but you oversee making your own choice you may think is best for you. Because God, our father in heaven, the Creator of all, has created us with our own free will.

Galatians 5:13: "For, brethren, ye have been called unto liberty; only *use* not liberty for an occasion to the flesh, but by love serve one another."

Key reference so you don't get lost in the road where we're heading, because God's not a God of confusion. But the devil is, and humanity loves to follow it. I strongly believe that if a dream comes from Heaven; it will be tied to the holy scripture of the word of God in the Bible. If it doesn't bond with the scriptures, that means, my friend, your dream didn't come from God, and that's the fact. There are three types of dreams through the fundamental biblical understanding, that the Bible describes, and gives provisions for, to confirm and back up his word. God speaks with humankind through dreams.

Job 33:14–15: "For God speaketh once, yes twice, *yet man* perceiveth it not. **15In a dream, in a vision of the night, when deep sleep falleth upon men, in slumberings upon the bed;"**

ACTS 10:10–11: **"And he became very hungry, and would have eaten: but while they made ready, he fell into a trance,** 11 And saw heaven opened, and a certain vessel descending unto him, as it had been a great sheet knit at the four corners, and let down to the earth:"

Numbers 12:6: "He said, "Listen to my words: "When there is a prophet among you, I, the LORD, reveal myself to them in visions, I speak to them in dreams. 7 But this is not true of my servant Moses; he is faithful in all my house."

False Dream

The devil speaks through dreams and uses different methods to pretend that God is the one who is talking to you. Remember, my dear friend, his actions are always opposite from God. I'm about to give you a quick method of a clear example. if you are sleeping or having a dream, or vision of having sex with someone, pay very close attention and let, no, one fool you or wash your brain by letting you know that is okay. Whatever he or she, said to you, what you were experimenting with from your sleep, was not from God. Above all, you were interacting and connecting with a bad spirit that presented to be your ex-partner, or someone whom you may have had a relationship in the past. It is not good for your health and soul, and for your physical body...! If any one of you who is reading this book is experimenting with this type of situation in your life, we recommend you please look for help from your pastor, or someone you can trust sincerely, to talk and pray for you. Also, you need to do your part, as well as to pray and fast.

Matthew 17:21: "Howbeit this kind goeth not out but by prayer and fasting."

Another one is if you have a dream that you were breaking into a bank or store and destroying someone's life without any meaning of self-defense. You are in trouble, and you need help to get right with God. My siblings, brother, sister, and friend, those types of actions, here are not from God. The Devil has always, been trying to imitate our Father God, he already knows, and we know it also, he will never be like our Father God, in heaven.

As I am writing this section in the book, my little brother, is explaining to me that a friend told him, that they know a woman, who says she has a dream of having sex with Jesus. If any of you for whatsoever meaning saw that in your sleep, remember, this is not from God, and came straight from the pit of hell.

1 Kings 19:11–13: "¹¹ And he said, go forth, and stand upon the mount before the Lord. And, behold, the Lord passed by, and a great and strong wind rent the mountains, and brake in pieces the rocks before the Lord; but the Lord was not in the wind: and after the wind an earthquake; but the Lord was not in the earthquake: ¹² And after the earthquake a fire; but the Lord was not in the fire: and after the fire a still small voice. ¹³ And it was so, when Elijah heard it, that he wrapped his face in his mantle, and went out, and stood in the entering in of the cave. And, behold, there came a voice unto him, and said, What doest thou here, Elijah?"

Ezekiel 13:6–9: "They have seen vanity and lying divination, saying, the LORD saith: and the LORD hath not sent them: and they have made others to hope that they would confirm the word. 7 Have ye not seen a vain vision, and have ye not spoken a lying divination, where-as ye say, the LORD saith it; albeit I have not spoken? 8 Therefore thus saith the Lord GOD; Because ye have spoken vanity, and seen lies, therefore, behold, I am against you, saith the Lord GOD. 9 And mine hand shall be upon the prophets that see vanity, and that divine lies: they shall not be in the assembly of my people, neither shall the be written in the writing of the house of Israel, neither shall they enter into the land of Israel; and ye shall know that I am the Lord GOD."

1 Kings! 3:18: "He said unto him, I am a prophet also as thou art; and an angel spoke unto me by the word of the LORD, saying, Bring him back with thee into thine house, that he may eat bread and drink water. But he lied unto him."

1 John **4:1** "Beloved, believe not every spirit, but try the spirits whether they are of God: because many false prophets are gone out into the world."

Dreams and Visions

Joseph in Egypt

We need to watch true dreams that come from God very closely, and pay attention like the King Pharaoh did in Egypt so that we do not waste time to find doubt what was behind those dreams. Most of the time some of you have neglected and missed the momentum of a powerful DREAM, God almighty has delivered to your life one time…! Pharaoh, King Nebuchadnezzar, and the King of Balthazar show us to never neglect the provisions of a Dream or vision we have, and not to give up until you find the true interpretation. God used Joseph, his servant, and Daniel, to interpret the dream and to glorify His Name in that period.

He then came before Pharaoh and told him that his dream meant there would be seven years of abundance in the land of Egypt followed by seven years of famine. Joseph recommended that "a discerning and wise man" be put in charge and that food should be collected in the good years and stored for use during the famine.

Genesis 41:1: "And it came to pass at the end of two full years, that Pharaoh dreamed: and, behold, he stood by the river."….!

Daniel in Babylon

Having related the dream, Daniel then interprets it. It concerns four successive kingdoms, beginning with Nebuchadnezzar, which will be replaced by the everlasting kingdom of the God of heaven. Hearing this, Nebuchadnezzar affirms that Daniel's God is "the God of gods and Lord of kings and revealer of mysteries."

Daniel 2:1: "And in the second year of the reign of Nebuchadnezzar Nebuchadnezzar dreamed dreams, wherewith his spirit was troubled, and his sleep brake from him."

Daniel 2:10: "¹⁰**The Chaldeans answered before the king, and said, There is not a man upon the earth that can shew the king's matter: therefore *there is* no king, lord, nor ruler, *that* asked such things at any magician, or astrologer, or Chaldean.**"

Daniel 2:20–23: "²⁰Daniel answered and said, Blessed be the name of God for ever and ever: for wisdom and might are his: ²¹And he changeth the times and the seasons: he removeth kings, and setteth up kings: he giveth wisdom unto the wise, and knowledge to them that know understanding: ²²He revealeth the deep and secret things: he knoweth what *is* in the darkness, and the light dwelleth with him. ²³**I thank thee, and praise thee, O thou God of my fathers, who hast given me wisdom and**

might, and hast made known unto me now what we desired of thee: for thou hast *now* made known unto us the king's matter."

Daniel 2:44–47: "**⁴⁴And in the days of these kings shall the God of heaven set up a kingdom, which shall never be destroyed: and the kingdom shall not be left to other people, *but* it shall break in pieces and consume all these kingdoms, and it shall stand for ever.** ⁴⁵Forasmuch as thou sawest that the stone was cut out of the mountain without hands, and that it brake in pieces the iron, the brass, the clay, the silver, and the gold; the great God hath made known to the king what shall come to pass hereafter: and the dream *is* certain, and the interpretation thereof sure. ⁴⁶Then the king Nebuchadnezzar fell upon his face, and worshipped Daniel, and commanded that they should offer an oblation and sweet odours unto him. ⁴⁷The king answered unto Daniel, and said, Of a truth *it is*, that your God *is* a God of gods, and a Lord of kings, and a revealer of secrets, seeing thou couldest reveal this secret."

2 Corinthians 10:5: "Casting down imaginations, and every high thing that exalteth itself against the knowledge of God, and bringing into captivity every thought to the obedience of Christ;"

Zechariah 10:2: "For the idols have spoken vanity, and the diviners have seen a lie, and have told false dreams;

they comfort in vain: therefore they went their way as a flock, they were troubled, because there was no shepherd."

Mark 7:21–23: "From within, out of the heart of men, proceed evil thoughts, adulteries, fornications, murders, 22 Thefts, covetousness, wickedness, deceit, lasciviousness, an evil eye, blasphemy, pride, foolishness: 23 All these evil things come from within, and defile the man."

Jeremiah 14:14: "Then the LORD said unto me, the prophets prophesy lie in my name: I sent them not, neither have I commanded them, neither spake unto them: they prophesy unto you a false vision and divination, and the deceit of their heart."

The Bible warns and rebukes in the book of Revelation those who enjoy adding and loving to take pleasure of taking out from his word. We have unwelcome news for you. You will face all the consequences the Bible reserved for those who break the law of God, and disobey his word. The Bible in the book of Revelation talks about the multitudes of people being in the water, and what they represent to the world. Also, those people in the sea that I saw on the top of this "IMMENSE WAVE;" also the same thing, the book of Revelation is pointing to us, the nation king, leaders, and his people.

Revelation 17:12–15: "And the ten horns which thou sawest are ten kings, which have received no kingdom as yet; but receive power as kings one hour with the beast. 13 These have one mind and shall give their power and strength unto the beast. 14 These shall make war with the Lamb, and the Lamb shall overcome them: for he is Lord of lords, and King of kings: and they that are with him are called, and chosen, and faithful. 15 **And he saith unto me, The waters which thou sawest, where the whore sitteth, are peoples, and multitudes, and nations, and tongues."**

Sometimes, we wake up in the middle of a dream or a vision and we don't know the interpretation. Then, we panic. Don't worry, because it didn't happen to you only. Prophet Daniel and Apostles John and Peter also went through the same process and were concerned also of the vision they were receiving from God, etc.

Daniel 7:15: "I Daniel was grieved in my spirit amid my body, and the visions of my head troubled me."

Revelation 1:17: "And when I saw him, I fell at his feet as dead. And he laid his right hand upon me, saying unto me, Fear not; I am the first and the last:"

Acts 16:17: "This happened three times, and immediately the sheet was taken back to heaven."

While Peter was wondering about the meaning of the vision, the men sent by Cornelius found out where Simon's house was and stopped at the gate.18 They called out, asking if Simon who was known as Peter was staying there.

Jesus walks in the water

After I had the dream, I analyzed it very carefully and compared it with the dream the Apostles John had on the island where he was in jail. We concluded it was the same dream and message on a different level. It was in a format our generation could understand. Jesus revealed to John in the century he was living at that time in the format that the people in this period could understand. But today in our era with the help of the Holy Spirit in the name of Jesus; I receive the same dream, and the same message in a way we can comprehend. I believe God may give you a dream of what will take place in the world also, my point here is; that God doesn't have exceptions; if John can reveal what will come to pass for humanity on planet Earth we can be revealed also in the name of Jesus. What blew my mind was, what my pastor Timmy, told me when I explained my experience with God in the camp. He replied to me that about ten years ago a missionary named Bob had the same dream on the same spot I had my dream! This is not a coincidence but a confirmation of God of what will happen shortly! We have learned from the Bible that the first wave of the show that took place was in Noah's time. Any source at the time which had something to do with water joined forces to create one of the first, big waves of show in human history. During that time, it destroyed all of humankind, and every animal, except those that made it to the Ark.

The second one was in Egypt, when King Pharaoh didn't want to let the people of Israel leave the country. The wave of the Red Sea wiped Pharaoh out with all his powerful army, pushed them to the sea. Before the Creation, the Spirit of God was floating atop the water.

Genesis 1:2: "And the earth was without form and void; and darkness *was* upon the face of the deep. And the Spirit of God moved upon the face of the waters."

What is the meaning of water? Water is a symbol that stands for the substance of life, in all its integrity. Jesus is the well of life.

John 4:10: "Jesus answered and said unto her, If thou knewest the gift of God, and who it is that saith to thee, Give me to drink; thou wouldest have asked of him, and he would have given thee living water."

We have been called to drink the water of life and to be above the water of trial, regardless of the circumstances we're facing in life. We must be like Noah in the Ark with his family. They were floating atop of the water in the name of Jesus. Remember also, underwater belongs to the animals who live there. Get out of where you are sinking right now. Yes, you can do it in the name of Jesus. "Wells of water" speaks of access and supply and much more in the Bible. When Israel traveled to a place where there was no water, God had miraculously provided water there.

Water is named 722 times in the Bible. Perhaps it is no accident that water is the only symbol shared by all world religions (22 March 2017. Wikipedia). Jesus walked on the water in the sea. Peter also walked on water, but fell and sank because of a lack of faith. Luckily, the goodness of the Lord Master Jesus, the Anchor of Anchors held him, and the wave didn't take him away.

Matthew 14:24–30: "²⁴But the ship was now in the midst of the sea, tossed with waves: for the wind was contrary. ²⁵And in the fourth watch of the night Jesus went unto them, walking on the sea. ²⁶And when the disciples saw him walking on the sea, they were troubled, saying, It is a spirit; and they cried out for fear. **²⁷But straightway Jesus spake unto them, saying, Be of good cheer; it is I; be not afraid.** ²⁸And Peter answered him and said, Lord, if it be thou, bid me come unto thee on the water. ²⁹And he said, Come. And when Peter was come down out of the ship, he walked on the water, to go to Jesus. ³⁰But when he saw the wind boisterous, he was afraid; and beginning to sink, he cried, saying, Lord, save me."

Can we imagine and think for a second for all of those who don't want to do anything with God, or anchor themselves in Jesus Christ? It is not a joke, because Satan will roll all of them over. The antichrist, throughout the satanic project, was proclaimed as the devil. That will come to pass soon and sink most of the world with him and all his accomplices' rebellion.

The Book of Revelation was written on Patmos. The Island of Patmos has been celebrated for almost the last 2,000 years as the place where the Divine and God-inspired Book of Revelation was written by Saint John, one of the twelve apostles of Jesus Christ. Wikipedia.

The Bible said that the multitudes of people that John saw in the water were of different nations and people who spoke other languages.

Revelation 17:15: "And he saith unto me, the waters which thou sawest, where the whore sitteth, are peoples, and multitudes, and nations, and tongues."

Without a doubt, we can confirm to you through the scriptures the multitudes of the people that we saw at the top of the wave of the show represent their nation, their languages, and their countries around the world.

Everyone that was there was representing their country. There were allies and, at the same time, people who formed part of the coalitions of the Third War machine system that has been already in place for decades and moving forward with the agenda for the Third War that will lead to Armageddon.

In this war, nobody will be the winner. The winner here will be those who walked with Jesus' faithful from day one, have repented from their wicked sin, and given their soul to Jesus Christ. Regardless of what did happen to you while you were on earth, nothing can be compared with the peace that will be granted to you in the eternity of God, one day in the name of Jesus, forever and ever. Mankind is about to face its self-destruction they were preparing with their hand. Mankind will not escape from this wave of bloodshed because of their evil abomination, their egos, and the stupid world they have been fighting for. Be careful. If you are not careful, you can end in hell forever. We were rolling towards hell, but thanks to our Jesus Christ, He saved us right on the edge, of hell. A lot of people without Jesus have disappeared and gone away forever. After death, it will make no difference if you are already in hell and repenting. It will be too late. Please don't be foolish. Guess what, friend. Every one of us one day soon or later will face God Almighty in eternity, imperative at the end of time...! Then you will find doubt and realize how much time you wasted and the little game you were playing with yourself and God;

that you are untroubled is not a joke, and is more serious than your little thought. And for all of those fights you were doing for earth power, money for women, etc. was not worth it at all to fight for.

The good thing is that if you are still alive on earth, you have all the opportunities in the world to get right with the Creator of heaven on earth. Remember! After death everything is over, you can cry and mummer all you want in hell. The Bible tells us about the rich man who was calling for help, Father Abraham, to come to help him but it was too late… earth is the perfect ground test, that God had prepared for a great reason before the foundation of the world, to try our faith, and if we passed the test; we will be reward also, in heaven and Earth forever and ever, in the name of Jesus. HELL, there will be no awards or rewards. I hope you got that noticeably clear in your mind. Both you and I let fight through the end in the name of Jesus to make it to heaven. God bless you; we're counting on you…!

God is a fair God.

Destiny has been the path to reveal our true position from the eternal and, to the end of Earth of who we are, and who we will be from day one from the beginning and, to the end. God's holiness is pure and transparent from eternity to the end of the Earth. Lucifer and his rebel angels in heaven had their chance but, didn't make it why that? Because they preferred the dark side instead of the light of light. The reverse side also will be the same for humankind, if choosing the same path, of the dark side, of the devil, this is where you will end up in hell. I'm taking you to another dimension, please be patient and pay very close attention. This is, a strong message, is from God, and I would like for you to catch, it with the help, of the Holy Spirit. When God was talking, to Jeremiah, and said, I knew thee, from the womb, of the belly of your mother, before you were born. God is talking to the world and, revealing his plan to you and me, that this prophet will go to a lot and that belong to him from end to end.

Jeremiah 1:5: "Before I formed thee in the belly I knew thee, and before thou camest forth out of the womb I sanctified thee, and I ordained thee a prophet unto the nations."

Wait we're going somewhere with you, and thank you for your patience. God says to Satan, "Do you see my servant Job and man who fear God?" We all know the response the Devil gives to our Father in heaven.

Job 1:7–9: "And **the LORD said unto Satan, Whence comest thou? Then Satan answered the LORD, and said, From going to and fro in the earth, and from walking up and down in it.** 8 And the LORD said unto Satan, Hast thou considered my servant Job, that *there is* none like him in the earth, a perfect and an upright man, one that feareth God, and escheweth evil? 9 Then Satan answered the LORD, and said, Doth Job fear God for nought?"

Remember when God Almighty told Abraham to sacrifice Isaac to Him? He followed the protocol of God and did exactly what God had asked for.

Genesis 22:9–12: "^{9}And they came to the place which God had told him of; and Abraham built an altar there, and laid the wood in order, and bound Isaac his son, and laid him on the altar upon the wood. 10 And Abraham stretched forth his hand, and took the knife to slay his son. 11 And **the angel of the LORD called unto him out of heaven, and said, Abraham, Abraham: and he said, Here *am* I.** 12 And he said, Lay not thine hand upon the lad, neither do thou anything unto him: for now I know that thou fearest God, seeing thou hast not withheld thy son, thine only *son* from me."

We can see here in the mirror of eternity, that God is revealing His desire for everyone to serve Him like to the world. This is the way it is supposed to be, and Heaven and also Earth. He knew who we are, and what would come to pass when dealing with all of us, including the angels…!

I have a sample question for you as you are reading this book, my friend. Which home do you choose

69

for eternity? Say whatsoever, that God doesn't exist, or believe whatever you want. One day, eternity will reveal itself to you one way or another. You will find doubt for yourself, rebelling against the power of God and challenging His character. That is a great consequence behind it that no one can manage it. Odule Bitol.

Luke 16:23–26: "And **in hell he lift up his eyes, being in torments, and seeth Abraham afar off, and Lazarus in his bosom.** 24 And he cried and said, Father Abraham, have mercy on me, and send Lazarus, that he may dip the tip of his finger in water, and cool my tongue; for I am tormented in this flame. 25 But Abraham said, Son, remember that thou in thy lifetime receivedst thy good things, and likewise Lazarus evil things: but now he is comforted, and thou art tormented. 26 And beside all this, between us and you there is a great gulf fixed: so that they which would pass from hence to you cannot; neither can they pass to us, that *would come* from thence."

Mark 8:36: "For what shall it profit a man, if he shall gain the whole world, and lose his own soul?"

On 6 March 2022, I had a dream. I saw that I was talking to President Vladimir Putin. I asked Mr. Putin, this question in the dream, "Would the Ukraine war lead to a Third World War?" He replied to me in the dream, that if they don't rebuild all the infrastructure, the game is over. When I woke up from the dream that morning, I was troubled by the dreams I had, like, the prophet Daniel, in the Old Testament. I didn't understand the dream. After the Sunday service, I rode together with my pastor, alone. We were heading to his territory home in Mississippi.

I told him about the dream that I had, and that I didn't understand it. Pastor Timmy told me that rebuilding the infrastructure meant that if the United States of America, Europe, United Nations, NATO, etc., don't retract from the sanctions they instituted against Russia, the Ukraine war can escalate and lead us to the Third World War! We can see before our own eyes how Russia, China, and their allies are moving forward with this new political agenda. The superpowers position themselves geopolitically so that they can take over the world monopoly. This doesn't look good for any of us. Everybody is struggling to control the world economies.

I had another dream. On 21 April 2022, I was fasting. During the fast, at about 12:30 PM, I took a nap. I had a great vision. One of Russia's most advanced warplanes was chasing a U.S. space shuttle. In the blink of an eye, the Shuttle landed at the international airport of Haiti, Port au Prince. I live 15 minutes away from the international airport. My house is in the center of the flight route of the airport. In the dream, I could see the Russian warplane chasing through the skies of Haiti, above my home. In the dream, I called out to my wife, Myrlene, that a Russian warplane was chasing the space shuttle. It was so real. The noise from the shuttle and the warplane was so loud it woke me up from my deep sleep. Instantly, I told my wife and explained to her what I saw. I looked at my watch. It was about 2:25 PM.

What, we understand very clearly, through the dream that we saw, is that if the prediction is right and lines up with the Word of God, with the help of the Holy Spirit, in the name of JESUS, Russia will soon be right in the backyard of the United States of America. Mark my words, friend! The old Russia, the Soviet Union, has returned to action on the same racetrack of decades ago, but in another political form. We can see how fast the new currency that Russia, with its allies, had projected for the world, is moving. The United States haven't responded to Russia, China, and the world. We know that Russia is one of the most powerful nuclear countries in the world. They would like to be the most world's most powerful economy. We can see more countries are joining the Russian and Chinese currency program economically! My understanding about the landing of the USA space shuttle in Haiti in the dream is that it may appear the United States has turned its back on the countries of the Caribbean and Latin America. In the end, those countries will be the only allies the USA can count on. Europe, Asia, Africa, and the Middle East will turn their backs on the United States of America. Author Odule Bitol.

Sometimes, we wake up in the middle of a dream or a vision. If you don't know the interpretation, don't worry and panic. Both Prophet Daniel and Apostle John were concerned with the vision they received from God.

Daniel 7:15: "I Daniel was grieved in my spirit in the midst of my body, and the visions of my head troubled me."

Revelation 1:17: "And when I saw him, I fell at his feet as dead. And he laid his right hand upon me, saying unto me, Fear not; I am the first and the last:"

The Bible said that the multitudes of people that John saw in the water were nations and people who spoke other languages.

Revelation 17:15: "And he saith unto me, The waters which thou sawest, where the whore sitteth, are peoples, and multitudes, and nations, and tongues."

Without a doubt, we can say that the multitudes of the people that I saw at the top of the wave of the show represent their nation and their country. We can move on and say that all of them that were at the top of the wave of the show form part of the coalitions of the Third World War and the big system machine of war that has already been in place for decades.

1 Kings 13:18: "He said unto him, I am a prophet also as thou art; and an angel spake unto me by the word of the LORD, saying, Bring him back with thee into thine house, that he may eat bread and drink water. But he lied unto him."

The Return of Christ

This current wave of war between Russia, Ukraine, China, Taiwan, North Korea and South Korea, Iran, Siria, Palestine, and Afghanistan with Israel, earthquakes, floods, tsunamis, etc., are the beginning, preparation, and sound of the trumpet for the Third World War. We should be ready, pay attention, and prepare for what's coming. The machine of the Third War is already on the march. Do you get it? Next, it may be China and North Korea that engage themselves in the war. China will go after Taiwan and North Korea after South Korea, their adversaries. Israel not playing and will fight with whosoever to the end and have God's backup. They are prepared and waiting for the right opportunity and the right moment to move forward with their agenda. What Russia did with Ukraine, my friend, didn't happen overnight. Everything was methodically prepared and calculated. In my dream, those who were on top of the wave were all kinds of high-profile people. I can see through the dream and caught this strong image of a very important political figure, like the president of North Korea, on top of the multitude. That proves to you and me that the ambitious political figures that we saw are not part of the solution. They will feed the conflict around the world. What's coming? This is not a joke. It's more real than we can imagine. It's time to get it right with the Creator of Heaven and Earth. Anchor your life in the throne of the living God, in JESUS' name.

Hebrews 6:19: "Which hope we have as an anchor of the soul, both sure and steadfast, and which entereth into that within the veil;"

It is going to be very bad news for those who are not anchored in God. There is no doubt about the dream of the wave of shows. Kim Jong Un's father left him a heritage. He has been working in secret to reach his gold. One day, he will reach it. Mark my words; when he does, he will surprise the world even if it may cost him a lot after he done it.

The wave of show swept all of them away. What we understand very clearly here is an invisible spiritual portrait that will materialize and come to pass very soon on this planet Earth. All those superpowers are going to put themselves together, executing their ambitions and agenda to fulfill their political lusts. They will use their so-called allies and influence their leadership to break the ice for them to go through. Trouble has started already. The world is about to turn upside down.

Our ignorance and season

I have a question for you, Who invented the season or created it? No one did. God's creation of the season, why that? because of disobedience! The proposal for each of these seasons is to conduct their mission in a specific period. Wait, because we're going somewhere with you. Spring, Winter, summer, and autumn, and each one of them completely one another. Spring, also known as springtime, is one of the four temperate seasons, succeeding winter and preceding summer. There are various technical definitions of spring, but local usage of the term varies according to local climate, culture, and customs. When it is spring in the Northern Hemisphere, it is autumn in the Southern Hemisphere, and vice versa. At the spring (or vernal) equinox, days and nights are approximately twelve hours long, with daytime length increasing and nighttime length decreasing as the season progresses until the Summer Solstice in June (Northern Hemisphere) and December (Southern Hemisphere). Wikipedia. The projection of those seasons is the eternal and earth packages in all their unique potential definitions and characteristics. The good news here is that God always takes care of us through all of those natural seasons, bad or good, and protects us. All of us at some point in our lives were navigating through a season of ignorance in sin but, God in his Mercy rescued us through the blood of Jesus. We pray to God almighty for you in the name of Jesus; to have mercy on you on his return and don't find you in the wrong evil season but in the right perfect heavenly season! Odule Bitol!

Genesis 8:22: "While the earth remaineth, seedtime and harvest, and cold and heat, and summer and winter, and day and night shall not cease."

Ecclesiastes 3:1–6: "To everyth*ing there is* a season, and a time to every purpose under the heaven: [2]A time to be born, and a time to die; a time to plant, and a time to pluck up *that which is* planted; [3]A time to kill, and a time to heal; a time to break down, and a time to build up; [4]**A time to weep, and a time to laugh; a time to mourn, and a time to dance;** [5]A time to cast away stones, and a time to gather stones together; a time to embrace, and a time to refrain from embracing; [6]A time to get, and a time to lose; a time to keep, and a time to cast away; [7]A time to rend, and a time to sew; a time to keep silence, and a time to speak; [8]**A time to love, and a time to hate; a time of war, and a time of peace.**"

Wave of Shows

There is no doubt my friend, some of you sometimes are expecting that things will get better in the world. I have bad news and good news for you. Which one you would like to hear first? Haiti's former President René Préval always liked to hear the good instead of the bad news. Sometimes, we all do the same thing but the reality is that we must deal with good news and bad news. If you're spiritually awake, look at your spiritual clock and see what time it is. I'm sure if you're not sleeping your clock will tell you there is no more time to be playing games. The end of the time is closer than ever before. My recommendation for you and your family: get it right with THE CREATOR OF HEAVEN AND EARTH. Look around for yourself and see what is taking place step by step in the universe. The whole world is upside-down according to the Book of Life and the Book of Books. And if you're paying attention very closely, everything is wrapping up slowly and faster than ever. Those who don't have JESUS in their life are scared and don't know what to do. Believe it or not, they know that everything is about to come to an end but instead for them to look for God they ignore the warning. The words of GOD are being fulfilled. Inch by inch, foot by foot, meter by meter, second by second, minute by minute, hour by hour, day by day, week by week, month by month, and year by year. No excuse. What is to come is not pretty.

Isaiah 55:11: "So shall my word be that goeth forth out of my mouth: it shall not return unto me void, but it shall accomplish that which I please, and it shall prosper in the thing whereto I sent it."

This time is not a time to be joking around or playing with your soul and your eternal salvation. Above all, you need to be seeking God according to His words more than ever before it is too late, my friend.

Matthew 6:33: "But seek ye first the kingdom of God, and his righteousness; and all these things shall be added unto you."

God, the creator of heaven and earth had created everything in proper order and a divine protocol to follow. But humankind chose not to do so. Instead, they followed their own stupidity and made it worse and worse. The reality is that we destroy everything that GOD AL-MIGHTY has created for our good with our own hands. Let's take a quick trip with you!

History will always be history, and nobody can change it. Humankind has done its best to change it, but we can't. History will remain the same, regardless of what they are trying to do with it.

The Bible teaches us about the momentous events that already happened in heaven. History will continue to talk about it from generation to generation...

The first wave of trouble happened in heaven, when Michael and his angels threw out the Devil and his rebel angels to the earth.

Revelation 12:**7–9: "**And there was war in heaven: Michael and his angels fought against the dragon; and the dragon fought and his angels, **8** And prevailed not; neither was their place found any more in heaven. **9** And the great dragon was cast out, that old serpent, called the Devil, and Satan, which deceiveth the whole world: he was cast out into the earth, and his angels were cast out with him."

The second one was when Adam and Eve didn't stay within the limits our Father God gave them.

Genesis 2:17: "But of the tree of the knowledge of good and evil, thou shalt not eat of it: for in the day that thou eatest thereof thou shalt surely die."

Genesis 2:22 and 24: "And the LORD God said, Behold, the man is become as one of us, to know good and evil: and now, lest he put forth his hand, and take also of the tree of life, and eat, and live forever: 24 So he drove out the man; and he placed at the east of the garden of Eden Cherubims, and a flaming sword which turned every way, to keep the way of the tree of life."

The third one was during the time of Noah, when God Almighty, the Creator of heaven and earth, destroyed every living creature that was breeding at that time on planet Earth. He left only eight people and some chosen animals to live and reproduce so the rest of the universe could know about it through history what GOD DID. The Bible said in the deluge, the wave went up to more than fifteen cubits above the mountain.

Genesis 7:8–20: "Of clean beasts, and of beasts that *are* not clean, and of fowls, and of everything that creepeth upon the earth, **9** There went in two and two unto Noah into the ark, the male and the female, as God had commanded Noah. 13 In the selfsame day entered Noah, and Shem, and Ham, and Japheth, the sons of Noah, and Noah's wife, and the three wives of his sons with them, into the ark; 14 They, and every beast after his kind, and all the cattle after their kind, and every creeping thing that creepeth upon the earth after his kind, and every fowl after his kind, every bird of every sort. 20 Fifteen cubits upward did the waters prevail; and the mountains were covered. 23 And every living substance was destroyed which was upon the face of the ground, both man, and cattle, and the creeping things, and the fowl of the heaven; and they were destroyed from the earth: and Noah only remained *alive*, and they that *were* with him in the ark.

The fourth one was the tower of Babel, where God confused mankind's language.

Genesis 8:7–9: "Go to, let us go down, and there confound their language, that they may not understand one another's speech. **8** So the LORD scattered them abroad from thence upon the face of all the earth: and they left off to build the city. **9** Therefore is the name of it called Babel; because the LORD did there confound the language of all the earth: and from thence did the LORD scatter them abroad upon the face of all the earth."

The fifth one was when God destroyed Sodom and Gomorra and killed everyone that was living there. Only Lot and his daughter made it out alive.

Genesis 19:24–25: "Then the LORD rained upon Sodom and upon Gomorrah brimstone and fire from the LORD out of heaven; **25** And he overthrew those cities, and all the plain, and all the inhabitants of the cities, and that which grew upon the ground."

The sixth one was when the people of the Israel went through the Sea.

Exodus 14:14–16: "The LORD shall fight for you, and ye shall hold your peace. **15** And the LORD said unto Moses, Wherefore criest thou unto me? speak unto the children of Israel, that they go forward: **16** But lift thou up thy rod, and stretch out thine hand over the sea, and divide it: and the children of Israel shall go on dry *ground* through the midst of the sea."

The seventh one was on the day of Pentecost, when everyone who were in the open room spoke in tongues and also in the languages of all those that came from different cities or countries.

Acts 2:4–6: "And they were all filled with the Holy Ghost, and began to speak with other tongues, as the Spirit gave them utterance. **5** And there were dwelling at Jerusalem Jews, devout men, out of every nation under heaven. **6** Now when this was noised abroad, the multitude came together, and were confounded, because that every man heard them speak in his own language.

Finally, the eighth one was when our Master, Jesus Christ, was nailed to the cross.

Mathew 27:35–37: "And they crucified him, and parted his garments, casting lots: that it might be fulfilled which was spoken by the prophet, They parted my garments among them, and upon my vesture did they cast lots. **36** And sitting down they watched him there; **37** And set up over his head his accusation written, THIS IS JESUS THE KING OF THE JEWS."

Question: who always started the promotion of catastrophe? MAN. Let's look at the Old Testament, to Noah's time. This great man of God in the midst of all a nasty, perverse generation, remained faithful to the principal value of God. He was anchored to the Kingdom of the Lord of Lords.

Let me remind you, my friend, that God Almighty is the Creator of Heaven and Earth. His GOVERNMENT is perfect, forever and ever. What was not perfect in Heaven was cast down to Earth because there was no spot there for them. Guess what, friend? Satan did not lay back and accept what happened. The Dragon, the adversary of God Almighty, me and you, is always busy and waiting for the right moment and the opportunity for revenge.

Genesis 1:26: "And God said, Let us make man in our image, after our likeness: and let them have dominion over the fish of the sea, and over the fowl of the air, and over the cattle, and over all the earth, and over every creeping thing that creepeth upon the earth."

You know the history already. Let's move on... Remember, God created mankind, and the Devil put division between men and God.

Genesis 3:7: "And the eyes of them both were opened, and they knew that they *were* naked; and they sewed fig leaves together, and made themselves aprons."

After sin arrived in the garden, man tried to unite themselves against God Almighty, instead of the one who caused them to fail. But God, the Creator of all knew all from the beginning to the end, and divided them.

Genesis 11:9: "Therefore is the name of it called Babel; because the LORD did there confound the language of all the earth: and from thence did the LORD scatter them abroad upon the face of all the earth."

Pay attention closely, my dear friend. Three subjects here are especially important. We are going to develop each one and help you understand with the help of the HOLY SPIRIT. There was a social ideology of unity when they were trying to build the tall tower on planet Earth. The same thing is happening today in our society. Little groups in the world have united to follow the same ideology of the past to try to control the destiny of the world.

But the Bible recalls that God planned it like that because they were foolish... And in the coming future, they will go to where they belong, that's hell. In the beginning, God created everything and everything was perfect. Are you aware of it? If you are not aware of it yet, you will be by the end of this book. We are living in the last days and there is no more time for people to be playing religious games with God Almighty. My recommendation for you is to get it right with God before it is too late.

This book is called *The Wave of Show*, the preparation for the return of Jesus Christ. Some great or spectacular things have happened in eternity, and in our physical world. The Bible tells us from the beginning, and repeatedly the end of time it is closer than ever.

In Noah's time, generations of people didn't care about God and doing HIS will. No, they didn't care at all. We still are not paying attention to the warning that God carefully delivered to them through his servant, Noah.

In Abram's generation, people were doing the same weakness of sin. They didn't care, even though they had been reproved by the word of God Almighty. Believe me, my friends, we are not that much different from Noah. We are in the same boat. Abram was a good friend and pleaded with God for mercy for the people of Sodom and Gomora... God proved to his friend, Abraham, that He had mercy for them. When God spoke to them to repent from their weakness, they didn't listen. Instead, they chose to move forward with the rebellions against the KINGDOM of God Almighty.

The Bible teaches us very strongly through history that the MASTER OF ALL confronted a man named Job, who was living on our planet Earth, to teach him a big lesson. God let him know that His power is sovereign; and nobody can question what He is doing. The Bible says that God's project for our life is not for our wrong but for our good.

Jeremiah 29:11: "For I know the thoughts that I think toward you, saith the Lord, thoughts of peace, and not of evil, to give you an expected end."

Job 38:33: "Knowest thou the ordinances of heaven? canst thou set the dominion thereof in the earth?"

I'm about to ask you three questions. The first one is: Why are you among the planets? The second one: In what country were you born native? You were born to serve and represent Him with all your heart in your country and around the world.

Acts 10:35: "But in every nation he that feareth him, and worketh righteousness, is accepted with him."

The third one: what are you going to do to mark your passage on planet Earth? The first answer is that God, put all of us, on planet Earth to love HIM first, above all. And we must learn how to love one another without any conditions, and do what is right on the EYES of God.

Matthew 22:37–39: "Jesus said unto him, Thou shalt love the Lord thy God with all thy heart, and with all thy soul, and with all thy mind." 38 This **is the first and great commandment.** 39 And the second *is* like unto it, Thou shalt love thy neighbour as thyself."

The second answer is that God created each one of us on the planet uniquely with our own fingerprint and a strong perspective to worship Him. Above all, we were created to do His will and to serve our family and our nation and help other nations around the world. We were created to make a significant difference with your actions and do the best you can in your power to help protect and keep your country safe.

The third answer is all those faithful men who were living for God Almighty with all the heart in the earth have marked their passage. Think of Enoch, Noah, Job, Moses, Abraham, Joseph, Daniel, Nehemiah, David, Esther, Mudoch, etc.

Let's go deep and be honest. What is your plan to mark the world on the place where God has put you? Some have crossed to the other side of eternity. They left their bad heritage reputation for their children and their families; stealing, drugs, drunkenness, prostitution, rape, murder, etc. This is how some have already marked their path and footsteps. No, my good readers and my brother, sister, and my friend! We are not going to follow in those same footsteps. We can choose the better path, my friend – to do what is right and not regrettable in the eyes of man and God. It is incredibly beautiful when we choose to do what is right in front of the eyes of God and the world.

Now it's time for you to step up and fight back and take your destiny in your hands in the name of Jesus Christ. Mark your footsteps and passage in the presence of God. After all the research we have done, we concluded that the end of time is closer than ever. The Bible gives us a great picture of what has already occurred before and what will continue to take place in the future. There is no doubt, my friend. The world is about to catch fire and turn upside down. The wave of shows is getting closer and closer and is soon about to be unleashed on the earth.

Those who study the Bible deeply can understand with the help of God those prophetic pictures that the Bible describes. It's about to happen. God created planet Earth for humanity to live well and also in peace. However, man always find the way to destroy that happiness with his own hands.

What caused the First World War? I have a message for those who are the commanders in chief of nations around the world, who have the courage and take pleasure in sending soldiers to die in the war for no reason except for them to profit. If you don't repent from your evil weakness of your sin, without a doubt, the gate of HELL is wide open, ready and waiting for you. I didn't come to praise anybody here but to tell you the truth and what the Bible says. My recommendation to all of the kings, presidents, and former presidents and the rest of the world is to repent.

Isaiah 45:22–23: "**Look unto me, and be ye saved, all the ends of the earth: for I *am* God, and *there is* none else.** 23 I have sworn by myself, the word is gone out of my mouth *in* righteousness, and shall not return, That unto me every knee shall bow, every tongue shall swear."

United States, China, Russia, France, Great Britain, Germany, etc., and all of those, who think they own the world: you don't own the world. GOD DOES. United Nations, NATO, etc., all of you will be held accountable for all your wrongs.

Jesus came to Earth to conduct a mission. That mission was on the cross. He left to go prepare a special place for us to be with Him forever and ever.

John 14:1–4: "Let not your heart be troubled: ye believe in God, believe also in me. 2 In my Father's house are many mansions: if *it were* not *so*, I would have told you. I will go to prepare a place for you. 3 And **if I go and prepare a place for you, I will come again, and receive you unto myself; that where I am, *there* ye may be also.** 4 And whither I go ye know, and the way ye know."

That means He will come back a second time again. This time He won't be nailed to the Cross again. This time He will come to fulfill the promises He made to those that were faithful and anchored in His word. We are waiting for His return with all our hearts. Believe me friend, the time is coming when He returns to JUDGE us.

The wave of trouble is guaranteed to flood our lives. We may swim as hard as we can but will surely drown because sometimes, we forget that the battle belongs to God Almighty. Through visions and dreams, we can learn that what's coming our way is not fun. We shouldn't joke about it.

The Apostle Peter and his buddy, right at the heart of the middle of the sea, was going through a deep struggle through the storm. They were facing brutal waves, going up and down. They didn't know what to do. Their failing at first was because they were trying to make it on their own. How many times we have been there?, When we finally wake up from our sleep, we realize who we need to call – JESUS? Put everything in His hands!

Remember, as long as we are still on earth, we should never forget to testify the greatness of God, wherever we are, for what He has done for you and me. The solutions and the answer to all, anytime and anywhere.

The wave of trouble will always appear in our lives. Most of the time, when it comes, we try to manage our way out, but we always fall. We forget that we must hand over our fight to Jesus.

United States of America wakeup

In March…, I was getting ready to head to Haiti. The day before I left, I went to get my hair cut. At the barber, I was nodding off; I could not keep my eyes open no matter how hard I tried. I decided to go home to get some rest. I laid down to take a quick nap.

I had a dream. There was a big earthquake in the USA. Everything began to break down. Poles falling, cables breaking, destruction everywhere, and then everything became dark. When I woke up from the dream, it troubled me, so I called my pastor for advice on what was the meaning of the dream. He replied, "What you saw is correct. It's coming! The destruction of the United States is coming."

But the question here is why? The USA has turned its back on God. This is one of the central reasons this great nation has been losing its leadership little by little. The problem of my nation, the United States of America, and the world is not social or material, but spiritual. There is always a logical way to deal with social and material problems. However, when a nation ignores and rejects the greatness of God, the consequences that enter into the social and material conditions of that country cause it to fall into ruin. This comes from my book, *Haiti Return to God*. Odule Bitol.

The legislative of the United States, who make the laws, are doing their best to get the Bible out of everything. If they do reach their satanic goal, believe me, friend, the U.S.A. will hit the bottom. This nation will be in deep trouble. The former president of the United States, **George Washington says it's impossible to rightly govern a nation without God and the Bible.** And some of those who don't have brains are letting the enemy, Satan, play with them to destroy everything and their own country with their own hands. Believe without a shadow of a doubt: if the United States of America doesn't line up with God, they will be worse off than Haiti or any other third-world country in the world. Odule Bitol.

According to some far-right politicians and activists, the U.S. House of Representatives voted to outlaw the New Testament in May 2024. The bill is sponsored by a Catholic Republican lawmaker and backed by Christians like Speaker Mike Johnson and Rep. Tim Walberg.

The bill includes claims that Jews killed Jesus Christ, and some G.O.P. members believe that this would outlaw parts of the Bible. The bill has received criticism from both sides of the aisle, with some Republicans saying it could outlaw Christian biblical teachings and some Democrats saying it infringes on free speech rights.

The Religious Freedom Amendment (RFA) is a proposed constitutional amendment that would prohibit federal and state governments from proving any religion, prohibit prescribing any particular prayer, prohibit forcing anyone to join in prayer, prohibit discriminating against religion, and prohibit denying equal access to a benefit because of religious affiliation.

https://www.usnews.com/news/

Is this the time to play, or to be serious with God? I leave it to you...

Entrance to the U.S.A

I entered the United States at the age of seventeen to pursue a better future. I remember that time. You could feel the presence and impact of the power of this great country. But throughout time, the respect of that nation has been greatly diminishing because of the disobedience of the American people and their sin before God. This great nation was founded by God's pilgrims who left Europe, but the United States has turned its back on God. Now more than ever, the nation needs to return to the path of God because He is the only one who can make this great country, the most powerful in the world, return to being on the right track.

Values are gradually disappearing. In the past, Easter had huge significance but now it doesn't mean anything anymore...! This sacred custom is gradually disappearing little by little...! Before, there was a profound respect for the family statute. Now, we can see how deeply they are trying to devaluate it and replace it with the evil satanic statute. The world is going backward instead of forward...! In the past, there was free will to pray in the schools. This has been lost, and there is total disorder in the schools. Children are doing things that they should not do. That does not please God, parents, and the society.

Prayer was taken out, and weapons replaced it; prayer was out, and drugs came in; prayer was removed, and the angel of death entered; prayer was eliminated, and the door opened for rape, suicide, homicide, sex, and physical abuse; prayer was kept out, and teenage pregnancies were introduced. This caused absolute chaos in all aspects of the life of those poor young children. These things grieve me as a human being, a servant of God, and father of a family. So, can everyone understand what prayer means and our daily lives? Prayer is the vehicle through which man can connect throughout the "spirit" to express our feelings and our need to God and connect with His Kingdom. To receive all, the provisions and blessings from the Throne of God Almighty on Earth.

The simplest method for humanity is to be able to communicate with the Creator of creators to receive from above the strength and the supernatural power to combat all those evils that rise in our path. Man is not doing the things they were supposed to do before God and society.

Marriage is a big issue and is not respected anymore etc...! The leading nation of the free world has lost the respect and prestige we once had because of sin. When a nation rejects the greatness of God, automatic consequences enter all the aspects of the life of that nation.

As an author and minister, I can't remain quiet and maintain absolute silence. I would like to ask the nation of the United States, in the name of Jesus Christ; to return to the feet of God. Let us pray that God puts the right president in the White House and that he will guide this great country. Otherwise, it will get worse than what it is now, and the consequences will be even more serious than it already is. I am going to repeat the same thing I said in my first book: the problem of Haiti and the world is not social or material but spiritual. It is the same problem in the United States. God has blessed this country more than it deserves. This country must be an example for the world. If you are wondering why the United States is falling apart, the answer is truly clear. They are not following Jesus Christ and there is a lack of leadership. The Bible says that all the nations will bow down before Him. The United States is still the most powerful country in the world, but there is no leadership to stand firm before God for his country. So, may God have mercy and forgive the sins of this country. We should acknowledge the sins of our country and our errors before God. There will be other countries that would like to seize the opportunity if they can to harm the USA.

The United States is a country of opportunities. That is why I am addressing my American brothers, sisters, and friends, to step up for the right cause and to consciously vote for the right president, senator, deputy, mayor, and judge who are fit to do their jobs. Someone who fears God always does things according to the will of God. When a leader doesn't have character, no one has respect for you. When a leader has character, everyone follows and respects that leader. As a writer, I don't have a limit, but I can say from the bottom of my heart: it is not about the Democrats or Republicans but rather about the future of the American people and the world...! To work together as a formidable team to choose the right leaders, who love God and obey the words of God. Whether you agree or not, everyone depends on this great country in one way or another...! So, my motivation is calling out to the American people to seek God more than ever. The end of the world is approaching fast. There is no more time to be lost. There is no doubt about what I'm saying, and I say it with all my dignity. The day will finally come when we all will be held accountable before God. Let it be in the name of Jesus.

The Third World War

The ten horns the Bible talks about in the book of Revelation are the ten powers that will bind together to conduct this satanic mission on Earth. Three of them will be rejected from their team by the ANTICHRIST. It could be because they fill these other three horns, which represent their country's king or president, which are not useful for them anymore.

That smells like the devil right there. When he uses you, and thinks you are not useful for his satanic mission and his kingdom again, he will destroy you and put you aside. You will die slowly in your sorrow and torment and go to hell with him. Thank you repeatedly for our triumphant LORD JESUS CHRIST who is there to restore us when there is no more hope in life anymore.

I'm pretty sure some of you have been asking those questions when the THIRD WORLD WAR will happen. We are setting the foundation for you to give you the clue you need to know about what will take place on this coming day on Earth.

We all will start to see the preparation, and also the progress and process, taking place on Earth if we are still alive. But before the big explosion explodes, all who follow Christ will be out of here. Remember, the church is still here on Earth but, when the Holy Spirit leaves the planet, the universe will fall apart.

2 Thessalonians 2:6–7: "And now ye know what with-holdeth that he might be revealed in his time. 7 For the mystery of iniquity doth already work: only he who now letteth *will let*, until he be taken out of the way."

How many of you are waiting for this beautiful day? I hope you are too, peace and love! May the LORD guide you and protect your soul and mine too in the name of JESUS.

I think always about, what is going on around the world, may not be today or tomorrow but, for sure we know that will happen soon or later when, we all will hear the beautiful, sound of the trumpet, in the blink, of an eye, we all who were connected with Jesus CHRIST; will be taken away from this corrupt body from the world, to be with our LORD forever and ever. We are going back to where, we have belonged, from the beginning, to be with God, our Creator of everything. where God did set up our destiny forever and ever, where we will not see more sorrow, pain, sickness, agony, and betrayal.

1 Corinthians 15:51–54: "[51]Behold, I shew you a mystery; We shall not all sleep, but we shall all be changed, **[52]In a moment, in the twinkling of an eye, at the last trump: for the trumpet shall sound, and the dead shall be**

raised incorruptible, and we shall be changed. [53]For this corruptible must put on incorruption, and this mortal *must* put on immortality. [54]So when this corruptible shall have put on incorruption, and this mortal shall have put on immortality, then shall be brought to pass the saying that is written, Death is swallowed up in victory.

Our Father God says in Jeremiah 1:5: "Before I formed thee in the belly, I knew thee; and before thou camest forth out of the womb I sanctified thee, and I ordained thee a prophet unto the nations."

ALL the mysteries will be revealed to us when we are in heaven, with our dad, because we will be in the Spirit; and not in the carnal mind. Everything that was veiled while we were on Earth will be revealed to us by the power in the name of Jesus, and all the divine nature law of GOD. The intention and the purpose of God when He created humanity in His image and put us on earth, was for man to travel back and forth from Heaven to Earth. But sin in the GARDEN stopped the great project God did for us, we can scream with all of our lungs, and say without any fear.

THE LADDER OF LADDERS

JESUS is the ladder of all ladders. Through Him we will claim that LADDER to see our Father God! Jesus said no one can see the Father if he doesn't come through Him.

John 14:6: "Jesus saith unto him, I am the way, the truth, and the life: no man cometh unto the Father, but by me."

Genesis 28:12: "And he dreamed, and behold a ladder set up on the earth, and the top of it reached to heaven: and behold the angels of God ascending and descending on it."

Regardless of who you are, you will not make it to the kingdom of God if you don't climb the stairs of the ladder of trial. Many times, we have slipped or fallen from the steps of that ladder. But always, JESUS has reached his arm to save us and picked us up from our desperate situation to continue our destiny to heaven. Please tell me, you haven't had a slip or ever fall and just climbed the ladder on your own...?

For many decades, people have tried their best to interpret the BIBLE as they wanted. It doesn't work! The Book of Books has always spoken for itself and doesn't need anyone's help. It has come to pass that the book of Revelation reveals itself to those to whom God opens the eyes. Every piece of understanding is coming to pass before our own eyes. Odule Bitol.

Genesis 28:13–16: "[13] And, behold, the Lord stood above it, and said, I am the Lord God of Abraham thy father, and the God of Isaac: the land whereon thou liest, to thee will I give it, and to thy seed;

¹⁴ And thy seed shall be as the dust of the earth, and thou shalt spread abroad to the west, and to the east, and to the north, and to the south: and in thee and in thy seed shall all the families of the earth be blessed.

¹⁵ And, behold, I am with thee, and will keep thee in all places whither thou goest, and will bring thee again into this land; for I will not leave thee, until I have done that which I have spoken to thee of.

¹⁶ And Jacob awaked out of his sleep, and he said, Surely the Lord is in this place; and I knew it not."

Another World War is coming, and it will be the biggest World War ever. According to the Bible, one out of three people on the earth will die in this war of all wars! The prophecy is found in Revelation. 9:14–18.

Revelation 9:14–18: "Saying to the sixth angel which had the trumpet, Loose the four angels which are bound in the great river Euphrates. 15 And the four angels were loosed, which were prepared for an hour, and a day, and a month, and a year, for to slay the third part of men. 16 And the number of the army of the horsemen *were* two hundred thousand: and I heard the number of them. 17 And thus I saw the horses in the vision, and them that sat on them, having breastplates of fire, and of jacinth, and brimstone: and the heads of the horses *were* as the heads of lions; and out of their mouths issued fire and smoke and brimstone. 18 By these three was the third part of men killed, by the fire, and by the smoke, and by the brimstone, which issued out of their mouths.

At today's population a "third part of men" would be over two billion people!

A war is coming that will wipe out over two billion human beings!

In World War I in 1914, the death toll was 8.2 million.

They called it "The Great War."

With the founding of the League of Nations, we had hoped that this type of carnage would never happen again.

Twenty years later, 52 million people died in World War II.

With the founding of the United Nations, humanity hoped that the solution to world peace was at hand.

But the UN has produced no world peace.

There is another war coming.

There will neither be 8 million dead nor 52 million dead.

This war that is coming will kill 2.2 billion, forty times the toll of World War II.

It will be the worst war ever.

And peace will only be conducted when Jesus returns in his glory and destroys the enemies of God. Pastor Timmy Bradley.

Remember, the world has been mocking God for a long time. This will have grave consequences. Please let me share something with you. Some of them are ready to pay for the action, I wish they were not in hell but...!

"The King Who mocked God"

Isaiah 37 & 2 Kings 19

Assyria was a country in northern Mesopotamia in the OT times of the Israelite kings. It became a large empire. Sennacherib was its king from 704–681 BC during the reign of Hezekiah, king of Judah. Sennacherib means 'sin has replaced my brother.' He invaded Judah. He mocked God by sending messengers to Jerusalem to tell Hezekiah that God would not defend Judah. "Do not let your God in whom you trust deceive you …" v. 10 "… and shall you be delivered?" v. 11 Hezekiah prayed to God about Sennacherib's insults and mockery and asked for deliverance. God answered through the prophet Isaiah. "Because your rage against Me and your tumult have come up to My ears, therefore I will put My hook in your nose and My bridle in your lips, and I will turn you back by the way which you came." v. 29 At night the angel of the Lord struck down 185,000 men in the Assyrian camp. Sennacherib broke camp and withdrew to his home city. One day, while worshiping his god in its temple, two of his sons killed him with a sword. God is not to be mocked. Those who do, face grave consequences. On the other hand, as with Hezekiah and Jerusalem, He is mighty to save. https://calvarychapelwestoahu.org/index.php/announcements-mainmenu-85/word-to-the-body-mainmenu-127/1071-the-king-who-mocked-god

Marilyn Monroe (Hollywood Celebrity)

She had the perfect life that anyone could ever dream of; a remarkable amount of wealth and great fame, and she was astoundingly beautiful.

One day during filming, she was visited by Billy Graham during a presentation of a show. He said the Spirit of God had sent him to preach to her. After hearing what the Preacher had to say, she said: *'I don't need your Jesus.'* A week later, she was found dead in her bedroom.

The most accepted theory suggested she was suffering from depression and committed suicide. In fact, it was actually the right time for her to seek God, but she mocked God.

By Everett Collection/ Shutterstock
Thomas Andrews was inspired to build a ship that would be legendary during his time. After the construction of the mighty *Titanic*, a British luxury liner, a reporter asked him how safe the *Titanic* would be. With an ironic tone, he said, *"Even God himself couldn't sink the ship."*

The result: I think you all know what happened to the Titanic. **https://icytales.com/untimely-deaths-famous-people-who-mocked-god/**

Claim: A skit depicting the devil's triumph and a mockery of Jesus Christ supposedly during the 2023 Carnival festivities caused torrential rain to hit the state of São Paulo in Brazil a day after the performance, resulting in multiple deaths and widespread damage to property. https://www.rappler.com/newsbreak/fact-check/brazil-floods-not-due-to-mockery-christ-at-carnival-skit/

The **impenitent thief** is a man described in the New Testament account of the Crucifixion of Jesus. In the Gospel narrative, two criminal bandits are crucified alongside Jesus. In the first two Gospels (Matthew and Mark), they both join the crowd in mocking him. In the version of the Gospel of Luke, however, one taunts Jesus about not saving himself and them, and the other (known as the penitent thief) asks for mercy. Wikipedia.

Revelation 21:6: "And he said unto me, It is done. I am Alpha and Omega, the beginning and the end. I will give unto him that is athirst of the fountain of the water of life freely."

God will not tolerate to be marked! People wakeup because we are living on the last day in the world. One more time again the world is taking pleasure at the Olympic opening ceremony at Paris marking God Almighty. Who organized and plans the event with the partners they where marking God with their ignorance and Jesus with his disciples last supper. The athletics: was invited to come play and represent in their country. We have to be very careful about what we said about them...! but those who knew exactly, what they were doing and already has on their mind when, planning this event to marking Christianity. Marked my words Friend they will be great consequences all who were involved in the marking team. Believes me buddy they will be regret and pay for their wrongs doing like Brazil, when they mark God on the Carnaval. The whole world saw right before the own eyes the response God give Brazil, after the Carnaval. The results will be the same thing that will happen in PARIS in the level God will choose to do so...! Galat 6:7 Be not deceived; God is not mocked: for whatsoever a man soweth, that shall he also reap. Apostle Odule Bitol.

THE END

To finish my deep thanks to my Almighty God, the Creator of heaven, earth, sea, and everything on it. And my savior Jesus, my redemption and my triumphant forever and ever. Remember, my friends, your destiny is in your hands. It is not in someone else's hand to lead your life for you. They always will try if you let them…! God has planted the right seed in your life before the founding of the world. Don't ever give up on life with your goal and the dream that God almighty has given you. Let people talk about all they want; you just keep the focus on your mission, and don't be disturbed for whatever reason. Surprise the world and everyone when they were not expecting it.

John 12:17: "While I was with them in the world, I kept them in thy name: those that thou gavest me I have kept, and none of them is lost, but the son of perdition; that the scripture might be fulfilled."

The woman on horseback in the book of Revelation is a portrait of a vehicle that represents Satan and his Kingdom and his dominion over the heart of each individual human being who doesn't align with God and have a relationship with Jesus Christ.

Revelation 17:7–8: "And the angel said unto me, Wherefore didst thou marvel? I will tell thee the mystery of the woman, and of the beast that carried her, which hath the seven heads and ten horns. 8 The beast that thou sawest was, and is not; and shall ascend out of the bottomless pit, and go into perdition: and they that dwell on the earth shall wonder, whose names were not written in the book of life from the foundation of the world, when they behold the beast that was, and is not, and yet is."

That Devil has been riding the Universe for decades, including you and me, when we were still part of the world. He used to ride our minds and our lives how he wanted it and whenever. The horse is the symbol of a tool of transportation.

How many times did we, used to be Satan and his de-mon's carriage to go wherever to sin? Satan calls you his horse, but God almighty and JESUS call you my servant, brother, and friend. One day, God was gathered with his angels, and Satan came. We doubted the invitation, and God asked him where he came from.

Isaiah 41:8: "But thou, Israel, *art* my servant, Jacob whom I have chosen, the seed of Abraham my friend."

But today I thank God Almighty in the name of Jesus for redeeming my soul and saving my life from going to hell. I'm no longer a carriage for the devil to ride me like he used to do so. What about you my friend?

Wikipedia says, "The date of 4000 BC as the creation of Adam was at least partially influenced by the widely held belief that the Earth was approximately 5600 years old (2000 from Adam to Abraham, 2000 from Abraham to the birth of Christ, and 1600 years from Christ to Ussher), corresponding to the six days of Creation, on the grounds ..." So, now you have a clue of how long Satan has been riding this planet Earth as his horse.

Job 1:6–8: "Now there was a day when the sons of God came to present themselves before the LORD, and Satan came also among them. 7 And **the LORD said unto Satan, Whence comest thou? Then Satan answered the LORD, and said, From going to and fro in the earth, and from walking up and down in it.** 8 And the LORD said unto Satan, Hast thou considered my servant Job, that *there is* none like him in the earth, a perfect and an upright man, one that feareth God, and escheweth evil?"

John 15: "Henceforth I call you not servants; for the servant knoweth not what his lord doeth: but I have called you friends; for all things that I have heard of my Father I have made known unto you."

John 20:17: "Jesus saith unto her, Touch me not; for I am not yet ascended to my Father: but go to my brethren, and say unto them, I ascend unto my Father, and your Father; and *to* my God, and your God."

I would like to share my experience with you, for those who don't know how the satanic spiritual witchcraft functions in the world. In my youth, I was hanging out with the wrong friends. I know that when they ask you about voodoo, the first thing that comes to your head is Haiti. We recommend you read my first book *HAITI RETURN TO GOD*. The central theme is that THE PROBLEM OF HAITI AND THE WORLD IS NOT SOCIAL OR MATERIAL, BUT SPIRITUAL. Odule Bitol. There you will find out the real patrocinate of voodoo, where it comes from, and how it gets to Haiti...! We're touching a very sensitive, spiritual issue here about the woman on horseback. Without doubt, we can interpret it in many different ways. But the right interpretation is always in accordance with the Bible. I'm also teaching you from what I saw with my own eyes and my experience.

I remember when I was told we were going to a voodoo activity for the weekend. This happened more than thirty years ago. Now I know it was a satanic movement. When we gathered that day for our tendering ceremony, the person who was in charge called the devil. When the spirit came it was not pretty at all.

That spirit spoke from the mouth of this man. I remember his name until today...! He said in a loud voice and with a nasty tone, "This is my horse!" The spirit was mad at him because he hadn't done what he should have done to please him as the master. I want to help you understand

114

the spiritual package of the woman on horseback, without damaging any other meaning from its content. I also want to take you to another level you didn't know.

Pray this prayer with me if you want to give your life to Jesus: Father God, I know I'm a sinner and have been doing wrong for a long time. Today, I choose your path, instead of the devil's. Please save my soul and redeem me in the blood of your Son, Jesus Christ. God, I don't want to be the devil horse and carry anymore, and to keep treating me, like an animal.

Thank you for hearing, my prayer and saving me, in the name of Jesus. AMEN! Please don't forget to keep me in your prayers. No matter where you find yourself in the world, may the Lord of the Lords continue to bless you in Jesus' name. If we don't meet on Earth, I will see you in heaven one day, in the name of JESUS! PEACE AND LOVE! Author Odule Bitol.

The very simple gestures that you made without even realizing it or knowing it, invested, whatever the time was in my life. This has helped to build my character and be the person I am today. Through this book, I would like to thank you from the bottom of my heart in front of the whole world.

Thanks for your courage and for doing the right thing! My deep thanks to those who deserve to be thankful!

You didn't make it in your life, because you were so smart and had everything figured out. No, you didn't and neither did I. God was watching your steps and leading you day and night.

Thanks to all of you, my brothers, sisters, and friends, from the bottom of my heart, for your advice, courage and support. You were always there for me when I need-ed you the most. I will always remember the good, in-stead of remembering what anyone has done to harm me.

Most of the time we remember the negative things of the past, and never value the beautiful moments, that have pushed us to be who we are today...! May the Lord con-tinue to bless you and your family in abundance.

Author Odule Bitol.

La Mission Jésus est la lumière

Myrlene Bitol

My children

Medrac Bitol

Samuel Bitol

Sadrack Bitol

Abel Netgot Bitol

Michline Noel

Yrrelus Raynold

Suzan Cadet

Jean Zachary Cajuste

Joseph Jean -Louis

Arthur Tedrow

Patricia Brown (in memory)

Jemie LaTracy Brown

Faith Brown

Bernie Pierre

Asen Michel

Dany Marcellus

Elyse Marcellus

Harold Vital-Herne

Dasmain Joseph

Therese Marcellus

Emilienne Rabrun

Mary Head

Dinora Cortijo (in memory)

Guyrlene Clauvil

Jones Clauvil

Hans Wally Elmeus

Joseph Presnel

Williams, Deni

Victor Santana

Yves Barthol

Carlos Gomez

Jose Bazan

Souverain Derisemene

Marie Solange Ullis

Yvonne Lavilette

Rosenie Millus

Pastor Edouar Francois

Pastor Oscar David (Lawyer)

Pastor Jese San Luis (in memory)

Pastor Emanuel Revolus

Pastor Jean Charles

Pastor Alfred Jhonson

Pastor Jean Suis Gason

Pastor Timmy, Bradley

Jerry Woodley

Cornerstone Full Gospel

Larry Booker

Williams Pitts

Wyatt Woodrow Grantham

Cecil Williams

Donald Jordan

Charlie Brown

Harold Saranthus Jr. (in memory)

Barry Handerson

Walter Maples

US Coatings LLC

Pastor Rafael Almonte

Lorenzo Mota King Director Executive Social Service of Churches of the Dominican Republic Shepherd Christian Church of the Community

Guendolyn, C. Hayes (Fl Sentinel newspaper editor)

Pastor Ernie, Rivera, Former potential U.S senator for the State of FL.

Kimbely Loue for U.S Senate

Pastor Ezeqiel Molina

Curtis Graham Filmmaker

Doctor Moise Cavazos

Former Président Vicente Fox

Pastor Wilben Jean

Journalist Daniel Charles

www.ingramcontent.com/pod-product-compliance
Lightning Source LLC
Chambersburg PA
CBHW031427120626
46545CB00006B/2306